The Psychology of
Human Possibility
and
Constraint

SUNY series, Alternatives in Psychology
Michael A. Wallach, editor

THE PSYCHOLOGY OF
HUMAN POSSIBILITY
AND
CONSTRAINT

Jack Martin
and
Jeff Sugarman

STATE UNIVERSITY OF NEW YORK PRESS

Cover photo by Stuart Richmond (Voterra, 1994)

Published by
State University of New York Press, Albany

For information, address State University of New York Press, State University Plaza, Albany, N.Y., 12246

Production by Dale Cotton
Marketing by Fran Keneston

Library of Congress Cataloging-in-Publication Data

Martin, Jack, 1950–
    The psychology of human possibility and constraint / Jack Martin and Jeff Sugarman.
        p.   cm. — (SUNY series, alternatives in psychology)
    Includes bibliographical references and index.
    ISBN 0-7914-4123-7 (hardcover : alk. paper). — ISBN 0-7914-4124-5 (pbk. : alk. paper)
    1. Psychology—Philosophy. I. Sugarman, Jeff, 1955–   .
II. Title. III. Series.
BF38.M375   1999
150.19′8—dc21   98-21999
                                                                         CIP

10 9 8 7 6 5 4 3 2 1

Contents

Foreword

A strange thing happened on the way to the new millennium; personhood was discarded from the realm of actuality. The person as purposive actor and creator of imaginative possibilities; that is, the individual human subject, has been argued out of the current philosophical discourse. Personhood has been one of the central themes of Western philosophical thought, but it is now under attack on two fronts. On one front are the materialists, who have reduced personhood to neurological firings; on the other front are the postmodernists, who have decentered the subject and made persons mere performers of culturally manufactured scripts. A resuscitation of personhood cannot involve simply a return to the Enlightenment view of the person, but needs to confront the current organic and postmodern critiques of the Enlightenment portrait of personhood; and, at the same time, to advance beyond them. Such is the project undertaken by Jack Martin and Jeff Sugarman in their *The Psychology of Human Possibility and Constraint*. Their work seeks to reestablish, within the current philosophical conversation, personhood as a unique and irreducible reality.

I want to use this Foreword to set the stage for Martin and Sugarman's work. Philosophy can be viewed as a continuous, historically developing conversation or debate about two primary questions: (a) the nature of reality, and (b) the nature of a particular aspect of reality, the human person. Participants in the philosophic conversation, even its most highly original thinkers, can be seen developing from or reacting against the thought of their predecessors. The focus of the ongoing conversation has shifted at various times to different specific problems. Of current interest is the problem of whether the nature of reality is basically unchanging or changing. This debate can be called the form-flux debate. Those supporting the notion that reality is form believe in an absolute, unchanging reality, and the experience of change and movement is illusionary. Those holding that reality is flux and change argue that the experience of a stable order comes from the use of concepts and language. Conceptual understanding imposes a stable order on experience and creates a false image of reality as unchanging. The current philosophical conversation has turned its focus on the form-flux question. It holds that the answer to this question is the prerequisite to answering other philosophical questions. The so-called postmodern contributors to the current philosophic conversation hold that reality is flux and change; they argue against the Enlightenment notion that reality is unchanging forms. Martin and Sugarman are on the side of the postmodernists and hold that the nature of reality is change and emergence. They agree that the description of human nature that was derived from the form position (e.g., Descartes) is wrong. But they disagree with the conclusions of those postmodern writers that personhood should be dismissed. Those writers hold that because the static ontology of the form view of human nature is in error, personhood itself is to be dismissed. Martin and Sugarman propose that the recognition of the reality of personhood is not dependent on assuming the form position, but rather personhood shows up within the flux position as an emergent, developing, interacting reality.

Because of the importance of the form-flux debate in situating Martin and Sugarman's work, the remainder of this Foreword accents some aspects of the debate as it has taken place as part of the Western philosophic conversation. Heidegger advised returning to the origins of the philosophical conversation—the pre-Socratic philosophers—in order to circumvent the culturally contaminated accumulations of historically situated attempts to describe the nature of reality. Pre-Socratic philosophy differs from all other philosophy in that it had no predecessors. It was the first to reject mythological accounts of natural processes in which movement and change in the world was understood as expressions of gods with human passions and unpredictable intentions. In its place, the Pre-Socratics sought to discover universal laws working within nature itself.

The Pre-Socratics were searching for a simpler, stable reality that underlay the bewildering and confusing appearances experienced by people. That is, they proposed that reality actually consists of essentially absolute and universal forms or ideas or unchanging matter (atomists). What appears to people as change is only apparent and due to human error; change seems to be real, but is only a shadowy fathom. Parmenides is often cited as an exemplar of the Pre-Socratic form position. He proposed that the unchanging, absolute reality is not known through the senses but only through reason. This idea has reverberated throughout the span of the philosophic conversation. Heraclitus is often held out as an advocate of the flux position. He believed that fire is the primordial source of matter and that the entire world is in a constant state of change. Heraclitus added to the being of his Pre-Socratic predecessors the concept of becoming; that is, flux. Although reality is basically change or flux, it has the appearance of stability. Heraclitus was also interested in understanding why what is changing would appear as stable; this question has been taken up again by postmodern writers.

As the philosophical conversation developed, the strong case for the form position was provided by Plato. Reality consists of forms or ideas, which are stable and universal. Everyday experience is illusionary. People experience through their senses movement and change and take them to be real. However, this everyday experience of change is analogous to seeing shadows on a cave wall and taking them to be real. For example, reality is not the many different triangles one encounters, but the form or essence of triangle, which remains the same throughout the various appearances of different triangles. Reality is like the axioms and theorems of geometry, it exists independently of any particular geometric drawing. The avenue through which knowledge of reality (that is, the ideas or forms) is achieved is reason.

The form position has held sway throughout most of the history of the philosophic conversation. The Enlightenment search for universal and unchanging laws of nature (and human behavior) was based on the notion that behind the experience of difference, change, and movement there are stable rules or laws that govern what appears. Reality basically consists of these unchanging, universal essences and laws, not the changing particulars of experience. The scientific method was designed to uncover the forms or laws that stand behind individual appearances; and knowledge of these unchanging laws would provide humans with power over nature. Thus, the Enlightenment agenda was to progressively uncover the laws of nature and apply these laws to shape nature in such a fashion that it would provide humans with a golden age. The goal was to use the knowledge of the forms or governing laws to stamp out illnesses, replace human labor with work by machines, abolish hunger, and establish an everlasting peace among the peoples of the earth.

Much of the modernist agenda, which assumed the truth of the form position, was accomplished. The alterations of nature, made possible by developing knowledge of unchanging, underlying laws, produced positive changes in the conditions under which many people now live. The modernist enterprise, however, also produced a dark side. Instead of a golden age, it produced the human suffering that resulted from two world wars and use of atomic bombs. The technological sophistication of scientific progress was used, not only to better human existence, but also to control and destroy millions of people. For many postmodernists, their controlling image of the outcome of the modernist enterprise is one of deteriorated, naked, dead bodies stacked up before Holocaust furnaces. This image overwhelms the images of people being healed through medical advances and of space flights to the moon and planets.

The dark side of the consequences of modernism influenced many philosophers to reexamine the assumptions about the nature of reality that informed modernism. In particular, these philosophers—termed "postmodernists"—challenged the position that reality consists of permanent, universal forms and laws. Instead, they recovered Heraclitus's position that the nature of reality is change and that the notion of uniform, unchanging essences and laws is the illusion. Heraclitus had asked why if reality is change, do people experience unchanging sameness. The postmodernists' answer is that it is the concepts that make up language that impose an order on the flux and produce the appearance of uniformity and constancy. Language functions by gathering together items that are essentially different from each another and treats them as if they were the same. For the postmodernists, the basic characteristic of reality is diversity and *différance* (Derrida's neo-logism), not sameness. What is real is the multitude of different triangles, not the single idea or form of triangle. Thus, in the form-flux debate, the postmodernists hold that reality is flux, not form.

The idea that reality is characterized by flux, not by unchanging forms or laws, although not the predominant position, had made several appearances in the philosophical conversation prior to the contemporary postmodernists. In the nineteenth century, philosophers had been concerned about historical change and how it was possible for one living in a contemporary culture to understand the texts of people living in prior historical periods. Much of the hermeneutic writings were devoted to overcoming the problem of how the meaning of ancient texts could be uncovered by contemporary readers. Hegel's solution to differences in historical

periods was to revert to the notion of a form that underlay historical change. The form governing the diverse historical periods was
a rational plan through which these periods developed until the
whole of history was one, absolute concept. Kierkegaard and others criticized Hegel for his form position and for not accepting
history as flux. The notion that people in different historical periods used different sets of languaged concepts to impose structures of sameness on what is actually difference was strengthened
by the reports from travelers and anthropologists who recorded
that the structures of sameness employed in European culture
were not shared by other cultures of the world's peoples. What
were held to be universal forms varied according to the time and
place in which the claims were made.

Postmodernists most often look to Nietzsche as their most
recent forerunner and agenda setter for their philosophy.
Nietzsche advocated the flux position and held that when the
artificial structuring of reality was stripped away, the flux was
revealed to be basically chaotic and its movements to be ran-
dom. Thus, what passes for knowledge is simply an imposed
order that serves the interests of a culture's powerful members
(Foucault). This position, which appears often in postmodern
writers, seems to be based on the notion that if there are no
universal and unchanging structures or Platonic ideas, then all
ordering is counterfeit and intellectually dishonest. An alternate
position was proposed by Merleau-Ponty. He held that while
reality is flux, the flux is not completely chaotic, but possesses
emergent structures. These structures are not universal and
unchanging, but come into and pass out of being. They are analogous to eddies in the ocean that swirl up for a while and then
disappear. Merleau-Ponty found support for his position in the
last works of Husserl. Although in his early and middle works
Husserl advanced a method—phenomenology—to uncover unchanging essences or ideas, he seems to have shifted his position
in his late works to the notion that these essences and ideas are
not permanent but undergo change. Martin and Sugarman link
their work to Merleau-Ponty's and the late Husserl's position.
They argue against Nietzsche's and the postmodernists' notion

that the real is chaos, and, instead, explore the ontological and epistemological implications of viewing reality as flux with processes of emergent and changeable structuring.

Of particular interest to Martin and Sugarman is the idea of the self. In the form position, the idea of the self is held to be unchanging, that is, it retains a sameness of identity through time. The form self is permanent and constant. It was depicted by Leibniz as a windowless monad, unaffected and unchanged by interaction with the world and others. Postmodernists, in rejecting the notion that reality is form, also rejected the form concept of the self. Many postmodernists conclude that as with nature, there is no stable, unchanging, real self underlying the activity and action of people. Notions of personal identity or unchanging self are culturally imposed. In place of the idea of a stable self, many postmodern writings view the person as simply a performer of roles authored by his or her culture. Unlike actors, however, there is no "real" or authentic person behind the role playing—persons are only the characters they play.

Thus, the postmodernists' commitment to reality as flux has led them to remove personhood or self from the philosophic conversation and to replace it with talk of neurology or sociology. What is currently needed in the philosophic conversation is a recovery of personhood, that is, a recovery of the psychological realm. Such a recovery cannot be a return to the form self—the unchanging, soul-like spirit, but, instead, it needs to be the explication of a flux self. The question is how one talks about and understands a nonstatic, changing personhood; that is, a reflective and purposive self that is open to its own inner emotions and thoughts, to other selves, and to the flux of nature. Such is the task that Martin and Sugarman have taken up in this book.

The task is a difficult one because in the West most of the conceptual legacy concerning the self and personhood has assumed that the real is form and the self is unchanging. Martin and Sugarman move to recover personhood from within the position that the real is a flux in which emerging and changing structural processes develop. They have had to search out those contributors to the philosophical conversation who have accepted the view of reality as process and change. In particular, they have engaged the American pragmatists (Dewey, Whitehead, among others), whose ontological position was that the real is process or change; and Gadamer's version of hermeneutics, which delineated how understanding was possible within situations of difference. Martin and Sugarman's agenda is twofold: (a) an ontological exploration of the nature of personhood as it presents itself as flux, and (b) an epistemological exploration of how one produces knowledge of personhood when it is understood as structuring flux. I believe that their book moves along the philosophic conversation about personhood by providing an original and sophisticated corrective recovery of the person within the outlines of the postmodernist commitment to reality as flux. Their contribution stands on its own, but it also provides the groundwork that other scholars can use to explore personhood further.

Donald E. Polkinghorne
University of Southern California

Preface

*I*t has been said ungenerously that psychologists are attracted to psychology because of their own pathological condition. If we could be permitted to substitute "existential" for "pathological," we would embrace wholeheartedly the resultant, more generous statement. While not strictly existential in either its content or style, this book reflects certain existential motives in attempting to understand ourselves and our ways of being and knowing as individual, psychological humans embedded in our historical and sociocultural times and contexts. Early in our collaboration, we shared a long-standing desire to understand the human condition, a commitment that previously had led each of us to draft and abandon manuscripts to this end when we had become too depressed about their inadequacies. Constantly fearing a similar conclusion to our joint effort, we nonetheless persevered in producing the manuscript for this book. Despite seemingly inevitable and lingering misgivings and uncertainties, we did not abandon this product of our collaboration, and eventually asked Michael Wallach and James Peltz at SUNY Press to publish and distribute it. We are very pleased that they were willing to do so, and that they and their reviewers pushed us to improve upon our initial draft.

We anticipate that readers of our book will share some of our personal motivations in pursuing an understanding of socioculturally enabled individual psychological development. We also expect that most readers will share at least some of our experiences and background as psychologists and students of psychology. What we hope to offer as a return on your attention is a coherent argument for understanding individual psychology as developmentally emergent from the basic existential condition in which human biological individuals are, to borrow Heidegger's term, "thrown" into pre-existing sociocultural orders. The uniqueness of our argument is our contention that once constituted by, yet emergent from, these sociocultural orders, individual psychological agents no longer can be reduced to, or fully determined by, their sociocultural and biological origins. Further, while always constrained by their origins and current situations, psychological individuals actually can achieve a limited transcendence that allows them to contribute creatively to their societies and cultures. We strive to connect individual human experience in the physical and sociocultural world to the collective construction, both historical and contemporary, of symbolic orders and ways of being and knowing, without reducing individual psychological experience and accomplishment to these ever-present, inescapable, and necessary sources and constraints. We attempt to make this argument both psychologically and philosophically, and to demonstrate how it might play out in an enhanced understanding of a range of topics that includes psychotherapy, education, creative innovation, psychological inquiry itself, and modern life in general.

We are convinced that we have gotten at least some things right, and are apparently willing to accept the consequences of critical reactions to those places where we may be shown to have gone wrong. In the process of writing and publishing, we seem to have assuaged some of those motives of our own that precipitated our work herein. We sincerely hope to stimulate related activity and work in our readers, some of which might eclipse our own treatment of the topic.

Some of the ideas expressed in this volume have been articulated previously, but much less fully and somewhat differently, in Martin and Sugarman (1997) in the *Journal of Theoretical and Philosophical Psychology*, Martin and Sugarman (1996, 1998) in the *Journal of Mind and Behavior*, and Martin and Thompson (1997) in *Theory and Psychology*. The support of the Social Sciences and Humanities Research Council of Canada (Grants #410-94-0983 and #410-97-1106) has been indispensable to the completion of our work. We also want explicitly to acknowledge the support and encouragement of numerous colleagues and students whose reactions have proved invaluable in honing our arguments and presentation. Finally, we express our appreciation to our partners and families, whom we forgive entirely for responding to our stated intention of coming to understand ourselves better with such dismissive quips as, "Yikes, I'm not sure that's a good idea," and "Better you than me." All is forgiven if not forgotten.

The Challenge

Overcoming the Problems of Dualism without Sacrificing the Psychological

In North American and European psychology, there traditionally has been a strict separation and juxtaposition of private-individual and public-social domains. Moreover, it has been assumed that the proper object of study for psychology is the isolated individual subject. On this assumption, psychological phenomena are viewed as the products of processes or mechanisms of change that are mental aspects of the individual. These processes exist within, but nonetheless occur distinctly and separately from, the natural and sociocultural worlds.

Of course, the strict separation of individual from natural and sociocultural domains in psychology owes much to the philosophical legacy bequeathed by Descartes (1637/1960, 1641/1960). Descartes claimed that there is a distinct ontology for human mentality that is given by each individual's capacity for rational thought and free choice, capacities that bear no necessary relation to the automatic sensations and impulses of bodily experience that he believed arise independently of rational thought. In Cartesian philosophy, mind and body are of different orders, with mind the sacrosanct realm of the individual—an immaterial reflective consciousness separate from a material body. Contemporary cognitive psychology, in particular, presumes the Cartesian dualistic metaphysics. Human thought and action are to be explained in terms of inner mental attributes of the individual, whose mind and mental development exist in ontological isolation from a metaphysically divorced, external world of natural and sociocultural phenomena.

In the latter part of this century, postmodern textualism and social constructionism have challenged the dualistic assumptions upon which most extant psychological theory and inquiry rest. According to such critiques, a host of problems issue from these assumptions, including difficulties in forging a defensible metaphysics, in explaining how knowledge can accrue from experience, in justifying a priori conceptual schema, and in posing mentalistic explanations without infinite regress. At a more ideological level, to believe in individual reason separate from physical and societal forces is said to champion an indefensible individualism. The general solution of both textualism and social constructionism has been to recognize individual psychological phenomena (such as self, autobiographical memory, reflective thought, and emotional experience) as embedded within a contingent, Cartesian tradition of sociocultural-psychological dualism, and to replace the classic dualistic construal, and the tradition that supports it, with different, less problematic ways of talking, writing, and interacting.

For textual essentialists like Barthes (1977) and Derrida (1978), the psychological self is a literary achievement. As textual constructions in an autobiographical genre, selves are cultural ideas realized through socioculturally sanctioned forms of narrative expression. Such strong textual essentialism is anathema to psychology itself because the phenomena of psychology disappear into an expanded, inescapable text. Social constructionists like Kenneth Gergen (1994), while no fans of dualism, are not entirely happy with such a radical displacement of the psychological. They argue that psychological concepts and accounts gain their meaning through their usage, not within either minds or texts, but within sociocultural practices and relations. For the social constructionist, it is to the sociocultural embeddedness of psychological discourse that we must turn. Such theorists do not deny that something is going on in the heads of individuals, but argue that social accounts of these psychological phenomena are either all that is required and/or possible. In Gergen's (1994, p. 101) own words, "We are willing to accept social accounts of people's manners, styles of dress, and forms of religion. Why is a similar form of explanation not sufficient as well for people's accounts of their personal past?" It is clear from his writings that Gergen is happy to extend this conclusion beyond autobiographical memory to individual psychological phenomena in general.

Our Thesis

We believe that there is an important sense in which these various antidualist reactions and proposals conflate individual psychological experience with plausible sociocultural explanations for such experience. What is the point in gainsaying the phenomenology of individual psychology even if its most adequate explanation may be found in sociocultural (including, and even especially linguistic) practices? Is there nothing of value to be gained by retaining something of individual psychology against the ever-present sociocultural fabric of human existence? In this book, we put forth a position we call "dynamic interactionism" that distinguishes between the mostly sociocultural origins and practices of human psychology, and individual psychological experience. We will argue that the nature of both societies and selves is emergent and mutable, as a consequence of their dynamic relation, and that the problems of classic sociocultural-psychological dualism are really problems that flow from its assumption of fixed societal and psychological ontologies. We also argue that the kind of emergent, dynamic psychological ontology we defend is required to account adequately for human innovation and change, and is compatible with a neo-Gadamerian hermeneutics that focuses on fusions among sociocultural traditions and practices at both societal and individual levels.

We present a perspective on the emergence and development of the psychological that incorporates much social constructionist thought, but which still leaves room for bona fide psychological phenomena of agency, intentionality, self, and creativity. The major premise of our interactionist position is that in order to comprehend the nature of psychological phenomena, it is necessary to take into account both the private-individual and public-social domains that mark our existence as individual and collective beings. It is important to note from the outset, however, that both these domains are encompassed by a broader context of human development. It is only within this broader developmental context that the significance of relations between the individual and the social in human psychology can be properly understood.

As seen within the developmental context, human sociality provides the possibility for, and imposes certain constraints on, the nature and genesis of individual psychology. At the same time, however, it is individual human agency that makes possible, and yet constrains, the conditions provided by sociocultural milieus. Focusing exclusively on the individual elides important social relational practices essential to acquiring the psychological tools necessary for constructing our experiences as individuals, and for forging our individual psychologies. If we are provided by our cultures with the means for psychological development, our psychological constructions cannot be viewed simplistically as the expressions of wholly autonomous cognitive processes. However, while the nature of our individual psychology and subjectivity arises as something of a cultural endowment, it also is misleading to underplay our unique individual sense of agency, our individual moral accountability, and our creative, transformative capabilities.

When we think and act, we experience and understand ourselves as individuals. This experience of individuality is central to interpreting our experiences and intentions as meaningful. Much of our existential condition is undeniably individual. There is little to gainsay the experiential reality of one's vacillation in indecision, fortitude in resolve, pain in sufferance, or exhilaration in discovery. On the one hand, a view that presumes such phenomenology as resulting solely from autonomous sovereign processes would be fallaciously ideological—an overgeneralization of methodological individualism. On the other hand, a view that abjures our existential individual agency and individual transformative powers denies the reality of our experiential lives.

With social constructionists such as Vygotsky (1934/1986), Mead (1934), Gergen (1985), and Shotter (1993), we contend that the individual arises from the sociocultural. However, concurring partially with the contrasting view, as represented by cognitive constructivists such as Bartlett (1932), Piaget (1954), Kelly (1955), and Mahoney (1990), we also contend that the individual is not isomorphic with, nor reducible to, the sociocultural. But, one cannot simply conclude that both sides of an issue have merit and leave it at that. Such a declaration is not an end but merely a beginning. The hard work has just begun—that is, the work of arguing and demonstrating how positions such as social constructionism and cognitive constructivism, with fundamentally different assumptions and metatheories, might be integrated or bridged has yet to be accomplished. Indeed, what really is necessary amounts to a new theoretical approach, one with ontological and epistemological assumptions different from either of the positions to be bridged.

In creating a metaphysics permissive of this theoretical bridging, we argue that the ontological status of individual psychological phenomena is not fixed, but rather, is both emergent and dynamic. This argument carries special significance for theories of mind and behavior. It suggests that the real problem with sociocultural-psychological dualism has less to do with the drawing of a divide between societal-cultural phenomena and individual-psychological phenomena, than it has to do with treating that which is on either side of this divide, and the divide itself, as fixed and immutable.[1]

Human psychological experience is not reducible to its possibly sociocultural origins. Reductive strategies achieve success only if they are ontologically informative in the sense of showing that what were believed to be two ontologically different things are actually one thing. In other words, the things themselves do not differ, even though descriptions of them do. Successful reduction is impossible if important aspects of adequate conceptions of things are lost in the reductive exercises. Such impossibility clearly is evident in attempts to reduce psychological phenomena to neurophysiological states. (For example, knowing the neurophysiological correlates of emotional experience tells us nothing about emotional experience itself.) But, it also holds for attempted psychological to sociocultural reductions. When Gergen (1994) asks why we are unwilling to explain psychological phenomena, such as individuals' autobiographical accounts of their past experience, in the same social terms that we use to explain manners, dress, or religion, he fails to understand or wishes to deny, that one's manner, dress, or religion are not the same as one's experiences of, or reasons for choosing or engaging, them. Whatever the metaphysical and epistemological problems of psychological experience and explanation, they do not deserve to be denied or dismissed in this way, unless there are better reasons to do so than to avoid postmodern philosophers' problems with sociocultural-psychological dualism.

---

1   In all of this, it is perhaps important to emphasize from the outset that we consider metaphysics to be concerned with the nature of things that are posited to exist. As part of metaphysics, ontology sometimes is taken to connote those universal categories of things that are considered foundational and invariate. Clearly, such a position rules out the very possibility of the kinds of argument we develop herein. In our view, it is a mistake to insist on a necessarily a priori, universal approach to ontology. Such a commitment precludes what we propose as a legitimate metaphysical possibility regarding the nature of psychological and sociocultural phenomena. If the very nature of such phenomena is seen to reside in their emergent, relational properties over time, the assumption of ontology as necessarily

What is made possible by the metaphysics we propose is a coherent holding of an essentially social constructionist thesis concerning the origins of psychological phenomena, without denying the phenomenology of individual psychological experience. On this account, the phenomena of individual psychology are constituted initially through sociocultural means, assuming only a prereflectively active, biological, human organism embedded in its society, culture, and physical environment. However, once emergent from these origins, psychological beings must be understood as nonreductive, intentional, and reflective agents. What is significant about this emergent, dynamic metaphysics is its suggestion that classic, modern, and postmodern problems of dualism are not resident in dualism per se, but in the dualistic assumptions that sociocultural and psychological categories are separate, fixed, and static. Once the ongoing mutability of psychological individuals and societies/cultures is recognized and understood as an ineluctable fact of their dynamic interrelation, the substance and advantages of the kind of metaphysics that we envision and propose come clearly into focus.

We hope to explain how humans develop beyond their biological and sociocultural origins to create change and innovation. Part of our strategy is to construct a powerful synthesis of the work in this century that has been concerned with this problem in, what we consider to be, productive ways. The other part of our strategy is to articulate, elaborate, and defend two core theses of our own (what we call our "shifting ontology" and "underdetermination" theses) that explain how the personal, psychological originates in the collective, sociocultural, but is not reducible to its origins. In doing both, we take a strongly developmental

---

fixed unduly limits a full metaphysical examination of existential possibilities in human studies. Thus, for us, a proper metaphysical and ontological examination of psychological and sociocultural phenomena probes the existence and nature of these phenomena without a priori, universalist prejudice. We anticipate that our rejection of this prejudice may constitute, for some, an abandonment of the very essence and purpose of ontological inquiry as part of metaphysics. In response, we believe that the metaphysical argument we make contains within it sufficient rationale for our ontological approach and strategy.

perspective that, while mildly dualistic itself, avoids the difficulties created by more radically dualistic, traditional approaches to our problem.

SOCIAL CONSTRUCTIONISM AND COGNITIVE CONSTRUCTIVISM IN PSYCHOLOGY

In psychology and social science, social constructionism (Gergen, 1985; Harré, 1984; Shotter, 1993; Shotter & Gergen, 1989) holds that psychological phenomena, from the ways in which thoughts occur to the ways in which we are able to conceive of ourselves as subjects, are at root conversational and interrelational. Psychological activity, viewed initially as a kind of conversational analogue, is seen to arise from, and to reflect our immersion in, discursive social, relational practices. It is through our involvement in such practices that we acquire, develop, convey, and confer upon others the symbolic cognitive tools through which we manage our psychological engagement with the world. The means for organizing thought and forging and expressing experiential and imaginal constructions derive from our attunement to relational practices, the most conspicuous being conversation.

The primary theoretical strength of social constructionism is that it provides a plausible account of the way in which individual psychology arises and initially becomes organized. The emphasis on the pivotal role of ordinary conversation and other relational practices in the genesis of psychological phenomena helps to demystify the source of emergent, agentic individuality, requiring nothing more in the way of biological assumptions than a set of primitive neurophysiological potentials to move about in the world of experience, and to perceive and remember some of what is experienced.

In contrast, cognitive constructivism, owing to the works of individuals such as Bartlett (1932), Piaget (1954), and Kelly (1955) presupposes a more atomistic view of psychological change. As a cognitive perspective, constructivism ascribes primacy to the role of the individual in learning and psychological development.

Constructivists conceive of hypothetical learning mechanisms or processes intrinsic to the nature of human individuals. These mechanisms or processes are believed to preside over the individual's development, serving to construct, manipulate, transform, and append the various mental representations and organizations that comprise the individual's cognitive architecture. While it is not unusual for contemporary cognitive constructivists (e.g., Mahoney, 1990) to acknowledge the importance of social influences on individuals' development, they persist in maintaining a strong separation between the individual and the social, construing individual psychological development as taking place against broader patterns of interpersonal, social, and cultural interaction, but not as constituted of such patterns and forms. The focus is on the individual and how she or he learns to negotiate individual needs and purposes in sociocultural contexts.

A major theoretical conundrum for cognitive constructivism concerns the matter of how individual minds comprehend or affect other minds, a question of obvious importance when considering any kind of psychological or educational intervention. This difficulty lies in the failure of an individually sovereign process of cognitive construction to explain how human beings are able to share so much socially, to interpret, understand, influence, and coordinate their activities with one another. How is the intricate coordination and systematization plainly ostensible in human social interaction possible, given an isolated, self-contained, individualistic picture of the process of cognitive construction? Moreover, there is the developmental question of how on one's own, without the resources of those discursive practices we employ reflexively to partition experience, an individual could come to develop a sense of self. Without such resources, it is difficult to understand how one could take up practices such as labeling experiences as one's own, and recollecting one's experiences in autobiographical fashion.

Social constructionism deals with these difficulties by revealing common social foundations for our psychological development and processes of thought. Individual psychology is grounded in, and enabled by, a shared sociality of conversational and interrelational practices. These practices are continuously reproduced and promoted by members of a culture. They constitute a form of life. We are thrust into this collectivity from birth, and we are constrained in many ways to develop within the discursive and relational context it provides. In this light, human psychology is shown to be much less sovereign, isolated, subjective, and individually relativistic than cognitive constructivism would imply.

However, social constructionism presents its own obstacle, one that holds fundamental importance for any investigation into the transformative aspects of human development and psychology, such as those central to psychological therapy and education. The knot is, assuming the constraint of extant sociocultural practices on what human beings can think and become, what accounts for variation or transformation in individual understanding, knowledge, and behavior? How is transcendence of conventional socially embedded and realized wisdom possible? Neither the strong possibility that the forms of our psychology are derived from conversation and other relational practices, nor the likelihood that such practices are essential to the collective evaluation and negotiation of new ideas as these are introduced to the public realm, answers the question of where new ideas come from in the first place. While social constructionism provides a convincing explanation for how we become *informed* with experience, understanding, and knowledge, it is wanting with respect to explaining how we are able to *transform* experience, understanding, and knowledge.

Indeed, a strong social constructionist reading (e.g., Derrida, 1967/1973; Gergen, 1991) would see human psychology as completely constrained by the kinds of conversation and social relation found in social experience. As merely a manifestation of conversations and social relations, especially as captured in language systems, individual agents dissolve into the dialogue and social roles in which they supposedly are created and compelled to participate. There is little of human agency here, only social relational, linguistic structures that by themselves seem to cause phenomena that give only the appearance of being psychological.

In this light, the transformative and agentic capacity of individuals appears of little relevance.

It is, however, extremely doubtful that individual agency can be made to disappear so easily. The problem is that this sort of poststructural social constructionism begs the question of what it is that social influences are acting to constrain. What is happening here is a fundamental confusion about the relation between social structures and human agency. Human agents are not merely the invention and expression of social structures. Further, social and linguistic structures are very much the invention and expression of human agents. These structures constrain the expression of human agency, but only by virtue of the fact that human agents apply their understanding of social conventions to assess the merits of their intentions and behavior. The power of social and linguistic structures and conventions derives not from their manipulation of passive human organisms, but from their use by human agents who actively adopt and interpret them in light of their own lives and circumstances.

It is true that the methodological individualism of cognitive constructivism occludes the sociocultural origins of human psychology. Consequently, cognitive constructivism misconstrues the largely social origins of psychological development. However, cognitive constructivism does recognize the importance of an active agent intimately involved in the figuring of its own psychology. While we exist in a sociocultural world of persons, a distinguishing characteristic of personhood is the possession of an individual agentic consciousness.

Individualism and selfhood are drawing a great deal of critique these days throughout the humanities and social sciences (e.g., Sampson, 1989). However, an important distinction needs to be drawn. Much critique of this kind attacks, probably rightly, an invidious sort of individualism that slights or ignores the collective aspects of human existence, severing us from an essential part of ourselves and undermining any genuine sense of community. Nonetheless, the danger here is that such critiques might lead us to ignore the very real, unique sensibilities and understandings we develop as individuals in sociocultural engagement with others. It is difficult to imagine any form of psychological theorizing that ignores the ineluctable phenomenal sense of agency and individualism in human experience. What is required is a consideration of this kind of individual experience within the broader context of human development, including the conditions of possibility and constraint that mediate the essential interplay between the individual and society.[2]

ATOMISM VERSUS HOLISM

In the more general theory and philosophy of social science, the positions of social constructionism and cognitive constructivism discussed above may be understood as instances of holism and atomism respectively. Holism is the doctrine that individuals, their identities, and their properties are entirely the function of broader systems of meaning produced by social and cultural forces. For holists, the individual is simply the vehicle through which culture and society express themselves (Durkheim, 1938). In direct opposition to holism is the thesis of atomism, which holds that the basic units of social life are separate, individual entities, essentially self-contained and independent. For atomists, all social phenomena and institutions result from the decisions and actions of human individuals (Popper, 1948). In their most extreme and oppositional forms, holists reduce individual phenomena to societal and cultural phenomena, while atomists reduce societal and cultural phenomena to individual phenomena.

According to a standard holistic view, culture equates with a complex of shared beliefs, values, and concepts that enables

---

2   In a recent review of Burr's (1995) introduction to social constructionism, Lagache (1997) asks why, to date, social constructionism has failed to hold a dialogue with the work of Bourdieu, Heidegger, Merleau-Ponty, and others who have attempted to employ theories of social practice, existential philosophy, and interpretive phenomenology to argue that human reflexive agency arises from, but is not exclusively, the product of social practices such as language. As will become clear, such a dialogue constitutes a large part of our approach in this book.

collectives to comprehend and direct their activities. On this standard view, society is the system that coordinates these communal activities. More recent versions of holism picture culture as a text whose grammar and vocabulary come to be read by its members through a process of enculturation that enables human individuals to become the persons they are. In all of this, society functions as a set of interlocking structures that enables the appropriation and internalization of culture without reference to meanings, intentions, beliefs, and desires. For example, systems theory draws no fundamental distinction between a thermostatic system and a social system in its nonagentic, strictly functional use of terms like "communication." By conceiving of culture and society as things that determine their members, holists leave little room for the kind of agency that atomists attach to the activities of human individuals.

However, a small number of scholars have sought to compromise the extremes of atomism and holism in a manner that leaves room for both sociocultural determinism and individual human agency. A compromise (bridging theory) that bears considerable similarity to that proposed here (with respect to psychology) has been developed recently by philosophers of social science such as Giddens (1984) and Fay (1996). The key to this bridging of atomism and holism is to treat societies and cultures not as things with formal causal powers, but as dynamic interrelational processes through which social and psychological practices are ordered over time. On this view, societies and cultures just are the dynamic working through of patterns of interaction among agents whose identity and relative position change constantly because of an ever-mutable sociocultural and psychological interconnectedness.

On the processural view of Giddens and Fay, the influence of societies and cultures consists of enabling and constraining rules and roles that require interpretation by those who act in terms of them. Without such interpretive activity, societies and cultures never would be realized. Societies and cultures provide "the conditions for the possibility of action and guides as to how actions are to be performed, but it is agents who produce and reproduce this structure by means of their activity" (Fay, 1996, p. 65). Giddens (1984) calls this interplay in which structures enable actions, and actions produce and reproduce structures, "structuration." Again, on this view, society and culture are not things but processes of structuration and its consequences.

The holist view of culture as a text to be learned exaggerates the power of any sociocultural tradition to inscribe itself on its members—witness the great variability in individuals within a given sociocultural tradition. It thus confuses learning with absorption. Human learning requires a phenomenology that includes the individual's interpretation and reinterpretation of sociocultural meanings. But, it also is important to remember that our sociocultural traditions are imposed on us in ways that we do not choose, especially during our initial contacts with them. Even as we develop more sophisticated, complex interpretive capabilities, our sociocultural traditions continue to enable and to constrain us. It is through this process of enabling and constraining, which itself requires the activity of interpreting agents, that our identities emerge, not through a deterministic holism that stamps us uniformly into sociocultural molds. However, such partial independence and indeterminacy also should not be exaggerated. "Agents become agents only by being enculturated and socialized into a particular culture and society—processes which pre-date them, and which continue to provide the means in and through which agents can act" (Fay, 1996, p. 69).

The views of contemporary philosophers of social science like Giddens (1984) and Fay (1996) are similar to many of those views expressed below. However, for us, the key to overcoming difficulties with sociocultural-psychological dualisms (whether construed as holism versus atomism or social constructionism versus cognitive constructivism) does not lie in abandoning any such distinctions. All that is necessary is that these distinctions be understood to reference emergent, mutable processes in dynamic interrelation. What this means is that neither the sociocultural nor the psychological can be treated as fixed ontological categories. With this metaphysics in place, the emergence of psychological phenomena in the life span of a human individual may be seen to originate and evolve within a process of sociocultural embeddedness, which enables and constrains the emergence of a genuinely reflexive psychological self—a self that continues to be enabled and constrained by sociocultural and interpretive practices and means. Further, sociocultural traditions themselves emerge and evolve over a much longer time line in dynamic interaction with the activities of a myriad of individual and collective psychological agents. In what follows, we summarize the metaphysical picture of dynamic sociocultural-psychological interactionism that is thus revealed.

2

Selves and Societies

The Metaphysics of Dynamic Interactionism and the Emergence of the Psychological

*A*n ineluctable condition of human existence is that at birth, humans are thrown into already existing societies and cultures that have evolved in a real physical world (Heidegger, 1949, 1927/ 1962). As biological organisms equipped with rudimentary physical and perceptual activity, human infants are capable of pre-reflective, embodied experience that consists of moving about in the world, and perceiving and remembering some of what is encountered directly, without the mediation of reflective understanding (Merleau-Ponty, 1962). Our acting and interacting in the world occurs not with the benefit of detached, pre-existing minds and selves able to pick and choose those social experiences most facilitative of our personal growth and development. Rather, our minds and selves develop as our existential condition unfolds and evolves. We exist first as embodied biological entities equipped with primitive capacities to move, perceive, and remember, all marshaled initially in aid of survival. The active, functional engagement that ensues is what enables psychological development.

The notion of a prereflective agency implies that human experience springs from being bodily involved and engaged with the world. We are not born into a world objectified a priori by a natural ability for reflexive thought. Consciousness, subjectivity, and our capacities for understanding and knowing, emerge not from an innate Cartesian individual mind primed for ratiocination, but from the fundamentally embodied nature of our existential involvements. Intentionality (i.e., experience always being of or about something) is entwined with our physical presence in the world and with the world itself. This prereflective but nonetheless intentional physical presence, existing and experiencing in the world, seeds the development of reflexive consciousness. At root, the nature of our individual engagement with the world has an inescapable quality of prereflective immediacy.[3]

The nature of the human condition is such that our bodies are instruments of action that enable the realizing of an agentic presence. Embodiment is the means of expression for our worldly involvements—our various identifications, intentions, and purposes. But it is not just that we are able to act. There is something more at stake. As human agents, we are existentially charged to act (Taylor, 1989a). We always are engaged in some sort of activity, exercising our agency in some fashion. Even when we are "doing nothing," in the ordinary language sense of the phrase, we still actually are doing something. There is intention and choice in our posture. There is a certain choosing of our disposition and comportment of our bodies. Even doing nothing is taking something up. Our existential condition as embodied beings necessarily requires an active stance toward our own existence and our world.

---

3   As Merleau-Ponty (1962) summarizes this central claim in his work, "We are caught up in the world and we do not succeed in extricating ourselves from it in order to achieve consciousness of the world" (p. 5).

We must act to live. To be embodied as an agent is to deal with various significances and to be committed to realizing particular existential projects in a world experienced as a milieu of possibilities and constraints. The world has meaning, but it is meaningful only to agents who actively structure their experience in terms of an intentional, situated, embodied existence in the world. Any reflexive consciousness that we eventually develop, springs from the prereflective grasp we have of the world and our intentional agency in it. We always are actively at grips with the world, as we go about manifesting our intentions and carrying out our particular projects. It is the existential condition of a prereflective embodied agency that allows individual humans gradually to become constituted psychologically by the sociocultural forms and practices into which they are thrown and obliged to participate actively.

The Dynamics of the Developmental Context

Human development takes place amidst relations with others in sociocultural contexts. Through our immersion and participation in these contexts, our intentional agentic capacities undergo dramatic alteration. Beyond infancy, human development into psychological individuals consists in the internalization of sociocultural means, especially conversational and other relational practices, as the psychological tools for thought. These symbolic practices are an essential condition for psychological development. They constitute a common developmental space, or medium of expression, for both the individual and the social. Acting as a conduit through which public-social and private-cognitive domains can intermingle, they provide the possibility for the reflexive consciousness that is characteristic of individual psychology.

Language and other symbolic mediational means that are sustained and promoted in a culture's relational practices augment our ability to conceive and act on our intentions and purposes. They illuminate and give form to significant aspects of our experience such that they shape and organize both our embodied prereflective intentions and conscious deliberations, ultimately giving rise to reflexivity—our ability to render interpretations and understandings of ourselves.

As Vygotsky (1934/1986, 1978) revealed, the nature of the relation between the individual and the social is fundamentally developmental. It involves transitions brought about by certain kinds of human practice that create instructive "zones of proximal development."[4] Intentional structures formed in our conversational relations and practices with others provide the basis for learning how we identify with, and relate ourselves to, objects, situations, experiences, and our own consciousness. From the onset of sociocultural influence, the acquisition of symbolic means provides for the structuring of a reflexive psychological space comprised of the expressive, symbolic practices of relation in which we inevitably are compelled to participate.

We come to instruct, motivate, remind, restrain, and evaluate ourselves, by appropriating and internalizing the ways others have instructed, motivated, reminded, restrained, and evaluated us.[5] As individuals, our psychological development proceeds by learning to treat ourselves as others have treated us in the in-

---

4   Vygotsky describes how these intentional structures are co-created in instructive interactions between a child and adult or more capable peer, such that the child receives psychological supports that promote and enable the appropriation and internalization of expressive relational means. In these instructive "zones of proximal development," the child's more capable partner supplements the self-regulatory role of the child, explicitly furnishing the symbolic means that the child ultimately takes up as psychological tools. The hints, directives, explanations, gestures, and other concrete conversational aids provided to the child, carry and convey the organizational forms for self-regulated thought and action.

5   The notion that a reflexive psychology is born of the child coming to treat himself or herself as an other or object also has been proffered by Mead (1934) and Bakhtin (1986). Bakhtin's analysis of the contributions of public conversations and relations to individual psychology also includes the important insight that the dialogic and responsive features of public conversation, which are essential to its form as an alternating dialogue, must be appropriated and internalized along with particular linguistic tools if thought is to manifest its conversational character. Bakhtin notes that conversation

structive interactions forged through conversational relations in zones of proximal development. These practices provide the possibility for human agents to develop a reflexive awareness of their intentional relation to the world and to others. However, concomitantly, these same practices also constrain individual psychology by licensing the ways in which human agents can talk and relate to one another. Such constraints derive from our condition as social and individual beings, and are moral and ethical, as well as linguistic.

Thus, from the Vygotskian vantage, the forms for organizing thought and enabling meaningful cognitive constructions of our experiences, our selves, and others, are embedded in, and appropriated from, conversations and other symbolic relational practices. Once appropriated, these means become transformed into psychological tools that individuals use to engage in increasingly sophisticated, complex forms of activity, some of which, like recollection and imagination, become more and more free from the immediate physical and sociocultural context. In turn, the emergence of these more complex, abstracted psychological capabilities enables individual humans gradually to construct progressively more elaborate theories of their contexts and them-

---

is first and foremost a social phenomenon. It originates with what takes place between and among people. As such, its make-up is relational and dialogic, rather than monologic. Our use of language always reflects its origin in interindividual conversations and the kinds of relations in which persons are engaged. The kinds of relations between conversational partners enable and constrain what is meaningful and appropriate to say, and how what is said will be interpreted and evaluated.

As Bakhtin further discerns, conversational practices are configured by conversants' active responsiveness and sensitivity toward one another. As agents, human beings are actively disposed toward communication. Listeners attempt to understand and interpret what is said so that they may respond appropriately. Likewise, speakers tailor what they say to those they are addressing in order that they may be understood and, thus, increase the possibility of obtaining a desired response. In conversation, we endeavor to attune ourselves to one another, interpreting, evaluating, and anticipating our conversational partners. Dialogic and responsive features not only are key elements in fashioning public-social conversations, they also are evident in the more private-individual conversations of thought.

selves. Understanding resident in such theories, when directed at ongoing participation and activity in the sociocultural context, shifts the nature of such engagement from one of unmediated, direct perception and prereflection to one of mediated, reflective consciousness.

The various symbolic and relational tools that individuals accumulate through their appropriation of sociocultural practices and conventions enable and constrain the personal theories individuals construct and hold about their experiences, themselves, and others. The knowledge, beliefs, and valuations that we extract from our experiences are interpreted and integrated into our self-understanding in terms of personal theories. In fact, our very experience of self is made possible through possession of a kind of theory.

The forms of the theories that we develop of our selves and aspects of our individual lives are fashioned from our appropriations of interactions in the social, cultural world. In developing our theories about ourselves, we identify with certain socially supported conceptions of personhood, and are drawn to act in some ways more so than others. Conceiving of ourselves as certain sorts of persons imposes limitations on the possibilities open to us. Thus, socially countenanced theories of what it is to be a person act to constrain the shape our personal interpretations, values, and beliefs can take.[6] Nonetheless, the substantive content and constellation of interpretations, values, and beliefs held by an individual, is something of a unique construction. Because of this underdetermination of personal theories by their sociocultural origins, there is a great deal of latitude in the way each individual uses a theory of self, or ideal of personhood, to reference a unique experiential history and reflect on past, present, and future intentions, expectations, and actions.

---

6 Charles Taylor (1989b) gives a poignant account of the substantive moral goods that underlie our practices and play a constitutive role in the psychology of self-interpretation and self-understanding.

THE EMERGENCE OF THE PSYCHOLOGICAL

With the onset of genuine reflexivity, supported by a theory of self as both object and subject, the nature of human experience shifts ontologically from preconscious, preintentional to conscious, intentional (Taylor, 1989b). Whereas previously, the human individual existed only as a biological organism immersed in, and increasingly constituted by, sociocultural practices and means, the human individual now emerges as a psychological being capable of acting with self-reflective purpose. While psychological beings have their origins in their sociocultural embeddedness, once emergent they no longer can be reduced to these origins. The experiences of such beings are not isomorphic with their past and present sociocultural constituents.

Psychological being thus involves coming to possess personal theories of self and contexts (Harré, 1984). These theories of psychological beings are underdetermined by sociocultural and experiential data, in a manner somewhat analogous to the way in which scientific theories are underdetermined by relevant experimental and observational data (Greenwood, 1989). This is not at all to say that the emergent psychological individual ceases to be constructed in sociocultural terms, but that such an individual is now a reflective, intentional agent whose self-generated interpretations are active in any subsequent construction.[7] Still subject to sociocultural constraints, the genuinely psychological individual, through the exercise of sophisticated capabilities of memory and imagination, interactive with a theory of self, now is capable of creating possibilities for present and future action that are not entirely constrained by past and present sociocultural circumstances.

---

7   A somewhat similar position is taken by Harré (1984), in his proposed extensions to the Vygotskian view of development. More specifically, Harré suggests that there is a process of "transformation," which, following appropriation, involves the agent's personal instantiation of experience in an appropriated form of discourse. Other extensions to the Vygotskian position proposed by Harré are noted later.

Reflexivity requires that we be able to extend our experiences, our thoughts, and ourselves into past and future situations and contexts. Our interpretations gain meaning both from our prior experiences as framed in personal theories and understandings, and from our purposive anticipations of the future. Making sense of things involves a capacity to evaluate the relevance, continuity, and discontinuity of new experiences with what we already know, understand, and expect to happen. Thus, we must be capable of tracing experiences and ideas over time, and reconstructing and concatenating them as recollections and imagined possibilities. We continuously are preserving and projecting something of the meaning gleaned from the episodes comprising our experiential histories and imagining their relevance for the present.[8]

Only by remembering and imagining elements of the conversations in which we participate are we furnished with the symbolic and relational tools we require to consider past experiences and previous learnings, and to entertain future possibilities. Imagination and memory allow us to grasp and reconstruct the significance of our past and present, and to project ourselves into the future.[9]

---

8   We refer specifically to episodic memory as identified by Bartlett (1932) and Tulving (1983). Memory thus conceptualized is a significant departure from cognitive psychological conceptions of declarative and procedural memory (Martin, 1993a). Episodic memory refers to remembering in our ordinary language sense of the term, "memory." These memories for events in our lives are historic, experiential, autobiographical, and laced with personal meanings, feelings, and moral timbres. The mode of knowledge expression and understanding in episodic memory is a form of recollective and projective experiencing that is permeated with personal sentiments and identity projects that betoken a distinctively self-referential and self-defining quality (cf. Singer & Salovey, 1993). Episodic memories are unabashedly subjective in content, and in the framing of this content within a subjective sense of time and space.

9   In contrast to the schismatic treatment that memory and imagination often receive in cognitive psychology, we take them to be inextricably interrelated. Memory and imagination coalesce in our reflexive deliberations vis-à-vis their inevitable connection to our present purposes and concerns. The

In the deliberations of reflexive consciousness, our memories of previous episodes and imagined possibilities enable us to
connect the experienced with the unexperienced, the known with
the unknown, the familiar with the unfamiliar, and the ordinary
with the extraordinary, creating a fusion of horizons of past,
present, and future in which learning and psychological development can occur. Memory and imagination provide ideational
access to that which is presently absent. The memorial and
imaginative capacity to bring forth ideations of events and phenomena (i.e., in their physical absence) into the expressive conversational space of reflexive consciousness enables us to draw
similarities and detect differences, to construct categories, and
to engage in the common kinds of reflexive activities with which
we all are familiar—mulling things over in our private-individual
conversations, probing for possible ways of interpreting, anticipating, and dealing with situations and phenomena.

By preserving and reconstituting ideas and experiences across
time, our recollections and imaginings allow us to evaluate and
identify reflexively with certain experiences, and to retain the
personal meaning and significance attached to our experiences of

---

past and the future are important to us insofar as they play a role in defining
the present. Our recollective returns to the past always take place from our
existence in the present. What we remember depends on the current situations and contexts in which we find ourselves. Recollection always is an
act of reconstruction in which the past is appreciated relative to present
needs and purposes. Remembering is an imaginative reconstruction in which
we formulate ideations from the past in the service of our present and
anticipated purposes, sentiments, knowledge, and understanding.

In this way, memory is a present-oriented imagining of what the past
was like. Memory thus might be considered a "species of imagination"
(Warnock, 1994, p. 132). The major distinction to be drawn between episodic memory and imagination is that memory holds a special relation to
what we understand as being the truth that resides in the actuality of
events. In the case of episodic memory, the ideation is believed to be rooted
in some factual experience in the rememberer's past. In contrast, while an
imagination may be based on, or a synthesis of, fragments of episodic
memories, imagining entails a kind of transcendence in which we are able
to construct images and ideas of experiences we have never had, and phenomena we have never encountered.

actual and imagined episodes. Memory and imagination afford us a spatiotemporal fluidity of mind that is capable of operating outside of the more rigid spatial and temporal constraints that exist in the physical and sociocultural worlds. As such, imagination and memory serve as mediational vehicles providing a temporal extension of meaning that aids the organization, intelligibility, transformation, and anticipation of events and phenomena. Imagination and memory also enable a kind of sympathy with which to interpret the intentions and experiences of others, thereby constituting an integral feature of our ability to develop as persons and selves. Memory and imagination are essential parts of our interpretive and reflective practice as human agents.

Interpreting and reflecting are concerned with comprehending the significance of our remembrances, current circumstances, and imagined possibilities. Our ability to grasp such significances by interpreting the present in terms of the past, or weighing the merits of alternatives by reflecting on the present in terms of the future, is furnished by imagination and memory. In their mediational role, imagination and memory thus provide the means for navigating between our experiences in conversations and practices, and the theories we develop about our selves, our lives, and our world. The memories we construct of the past, of the present, and of imagined possibilities, can be instantiated in our personal theories and employed to support current and future interpretations, understandings, and intentional actions.

Learning, psychological change, and creativity are connected intimately with our personal theories, identities, and the sense we have of ourselves. By making it possible for us to bring to mind what is presently absent, remembering and imagining lend some stability to our knowledge and understanding across time. Without this fluid capacity to collapse and extend experience across time and space, every experience would be unfamiliar, no matter how many times an event or object previously had been encountered.

By making the nonexistent extant in reflexive consciousness, memory and imagination provide for an awareness of temporal continuity. Memory and imagination fill in the existential gaps between our phenomenological experiences of self, enabling reflexive awareness of the enduring and unified nature of subjective existence. Without this capacity, it is difficult to see how we might develop any reflexive appreciation of the perpetuity or permanence of our own existence or, for that matter, any conception or understanding of temporality. Memory and imagination are the gateposts that open to the wealth of accumulated past experience in one direction, and to the call of future possibility in the other. The spatiotemporal fluidity afforded by memory and imagination contributes significantly to the underdetermination of our psychologies by our sociocultural experiences.

Experiences become the subject of our memories and imaginings through the allocation and appropriation of personal meaning. There is a flavor of consistency to the phenomenology of remembering and imagining. However, this consistency is a function of the consistency in meanings with which past, present, and anticipated experiences are interpreted and understood. Our remembrances are transitional vehicles for conveying and transforming the meaning and significance through which experiences become personalized. Many of our memories and imaginings do exhibit a characteristic stability in retaining the imagery, sentiments, and attitudes inscribed in the original episode. However, through transformations in meanings, memories of previous events and imagined scenarios can be reinterpreted and extrapolated to suit present and future purposes and contexts. The meanings of memories and imaginings are malleable and expendable as new experiences, interpretations, and understandings emerge, and as we acquire new conversational forms and linguistic tools for interpreting the meaning and significance of events and phenomena.

SELF

As reflexive human agents, we continuously attempt to discern the significance of things, and to forge meanings and understandings relevant to our particular existential purposes and projects. The ways in which we learn to discern significances and to construct and interpret our experiences spring from our status as social entities in the company of others. The symbolic and relational tools we come to possess through our participation in sociocultural milieus allow us to interpret and integrate our experiences meaningfully and to gain some understanding of our circumstances. However, our interpretations also are made from within the bounds of our unique individual histories, recollections of which provide much of the substance for our personal theories of self.[10]

In attempting to discern significances and construct meanings, we look for familiarity and relevance between the present and the past. As adults, in most of our daily endeavors we do not expend a great deal of conscious effort in grasping the significance or meaning of events. Significance and meaning are given more or less instantaneously by the prereflective understandings that constitute much of our capacity for engaged agency. However, we frequently are presented with the unfamiliar, or with inconsistencies between what we discern of the present and the prereflective understandings immediately given to the present by our pasts. In becoming conscious of such discrepancies, we implicitly or explicitly acknowledge that the repertoire of understandings on which we draw automatically, is in some way insufficient. This sense of insufficiency in our understanding, incited by irreconcilable features of the present situation and our previous experience, is the impetus for us to engage in conscious interpretation. The movement from understanding to interpretation is the seed for the development of the reflexive consciousness required for more sophisticated forms of learning, psychological change, and innovation.

---

10   An individual's theory of self is constituted in the ongoing attempt to integrate the recollections of episodes comprising one's experiential history within the reflexive framework of a personal theory, and to imagine possibilities for self (Markus, 1977; Markus & Nurius, 1986). As Polkinghorne (1988) describes: "Self, then, is not a static thing or a substance, but a configuring of personal events into an historical unity which includes not only what one has been but also anticipation of what one will be" (p. 150).

During the course of development, we learn to instruct ourselves in dealing with these sorts of discrepancy, in manners similar to those in which others previously have instructed us. Early in our development, others point things out to us, draw our attention to matters of significance, ask us questions, prompt us to bring forward or project our remembrances, and suggest possibilities for us to imagine by posing tropes, models, analogies, or descriptive scenarios with which to clarify things, to bridge the unfamiliar with the familiar, the relevant with the inconsistent. Appropriating and internalizing these strategies and ideas, we come to instruct ourselves. Presented with unfamiliarity or inconsistency, we learn to engage in movements of interpretation in which we attempt to understand the significance of the present and future by projecting forward our experiential recollections and imaginings. We learn to clarify things for ourselves, finding or contriving our own generative strategies and means.

In these circular interpretive maneuvers, the present, the past, and the future are brought together in reflexive consciousness as a flux of memories and imaginings across time. When meeting with unfamiliarity and inconsistency, such interpretative maneuvers not only can lead to an elaboration or transformation of our understanding of past experience, but also, to transformations in our understanding of present circumstances. Learning, psychological change, and creativity arise from this fusing of horizons—of present, past, and future; of the familiar and the unfamiliar; and of the relevant and the inconsistent. Throughout the course of our lives, new conceptions are required to deal with the emergent significances we sense in our experience and understanding of our lives. With the passage of time, there are changes of many kinds to which we must adjust. As we age, there are changes in the nature of our personal relationships to others, in the broader domain of sociocultural belief and practice, and in our personal physical, intellectual, emotional, and spiritual needs and purposes. The mutable and transformative nature of human psychology can be seen as a fusion of horizons that occurs when past understandings give way to, or are recast in the light of, new ones, as we attempt to deal actively with dynamically emerging significances in our purposes and experiences as genuinely psychological individuals.

The activity of such individuals includes a psychological self, complete with a mind of its own, that has emerged from the sociocultural, developmental context, a self which continues to be shaped by, but also with some limited potential to shape, that context. Thus constituted, the psychological self may be conceived as a relational unity. In a manner similar to that in which Giddens (1984) and Fay (1996) have rejected the ontological idea of societies and cultures as fixed things, self, under this construal is not a thing that undergoes various changes to its essential state. It simply *is* various theoretically enabled states of consciousness related in a certain matter. Such self-states come into being in the very act of reflexively self-referring (Nozick, 1981). In this way, it is unnecessary to conceive of the self as a prior existing entity. Rather, on this account, the self is continually created and recreated in interaction with others.

Each individual psychological being reflexively makes use of self-referring psychological utterances and means appropriated from sociocultural interactions and relations with others. The self is an ongoing, dynamic process of construction, a constantly emerging achievement made possible by appropriating the means to reflexively self-refer, including a socioculturally enabled, yet underdetermined theory of self. As such, the self is not a fixed entity, but a process whose nature is fluid and changeable depending on the sorts of self-referring practices available for appropriation in the sociocultural contexts in which psychological individuals are embedded, emerge, and continue to develop through an ongoing activity of interpretive self-creation. The self is an ever changing unity enabled and constrained by human existence and experience in societies and cultures—societies and cultures which are themselves dynamic processes in ongoing mutable interaction with the activities of the psychological individuals they enable and constrain.

SELVES AND SOCIETIES

That psychological individuals shape societies and cultures also is undeniable, another ineluctable existential condition (Heidegger, 1949, 1927/1962). For example, attempt to imagine contemporary Western culture on the assumption that individuals like da Vinci, Bach, Descartes, and Einstein had never existed. Would some others have undertaken exactly the same kinds of work with the same kinds of sociocultural results? Such extreme social determinism seems highly unlikely. By imaginatively subtracting the contributions of these and all other individuals from what soon becomes a rapidly diminishing sociocultural fabric, it perhaps is possible to glimpse a state of societal nothingness (Heidegger, 1949, 1927/1962). Societies as aggregates of physical individuals do not exist without psychological individuals. Societies as sociocultural constructions never would have evolved without the activities of psychological individuals whose feats of imagination and ingenuity, even while undeniably grounded in (i.e., largely constituted by) existing sociocultural forms and practices, are not entirely determined by such means. If this were not so, societies, even if somehow initially emergent, would be static, and such certainly is not the case. That some societies might place little or no importance on innovation or Western-style progress does not negate the potential influence individuals have to shape the practices in which they participate in ways constrained, but not determined entirely, by their immersion in relevant sociocultural values and means.

One does not need to concern oneself with necessarily highly speculative accounts of the evolution of the human/world connection up to the point of the emergence of societies and societally governed human nature to appreciate the force of the foregoing thought experiment. Nor, does one need to concern oneself with speculations concerning the precise physical, biological makeup of human individuals capable of undergoing the kind of psychological, developmental emergence within sociocultural contexts that was articulated earlier.[11] As interesting and important for other purposes as such speculative theorizing may be, neither is necessary to establish the two conclusions that (1) societies require psychological individuals (selves), and (2) psychological individuals (selves) are mostly constituted, but not entirely constrained, by sociocultural means.[12] Consideration of these two conclusions is all that is required to envision a kind of emergent, dynamic ontological condition for both selves and societies that provides a quite adequate account of the nature of human societies and psychological individuals.[13]

Selves need societies, just as societies need selves. A psychological being develops a self only because it is part of a community of other selves, past and present, that has constructed a public, social world of common symbols, systems, and practices capable of underwriting a pattern of interaction in which selves influence and respond to other selves. But, even while selves are essentially social, they are not closed, fixed entities. Selves are

---

11   Readers interested in speculative theorizing concerning the possibility that the development of self is a biological necessity for human organisms may wish to consider recent arguments to this effect by Kempen (1996). While claiming that the human biological body requires the development of some kind of self, Kempen insists on the inevitably sociocultural determinants of the specific forms of self available to individual humans. Kempen argues that the requirement for self is biological and universal, but that the form of self is sociocultural and contingent.

12   Bourdieu's (1980/1990) notion of "habitus," involving a dialectical relation between individual dispositions and social structures, also leads to the conclusion that individuals both structure and are structured by the social world. Habitus works through language and related social practices to construct the social world, but is not exclusively the product of language and social practices.

13   What it is to be social and what it is to be personal both arise within dynamic processes in ongoing mutable interaction. In addition, the psychology of any given individual is emergent in the life span of that individual, while the accumulation of the agentic actions of individuals, and the sociocultural consequences of same, means that societies and cultures are also in constant evolution. The upshot is that there are no fixed ontological

dynamic complexes that emerge from the interaction of psychological beings with each other in sociocultural contexts. In a very real sense, they are the sum total of the trails of activity and relations with other selves within societies and cultures.

The perhaps surprising "flip side" of all of this, is that cultures and societies also are not separate, fixed entities that stamp their mold on their members. As the ongoing interactions of their members, they have no power separate from the active participation of those they enable and constrain. Cultures and societies are forever changing by virtue of the activities of their members.[14] Creativity and innovation unfold at the confluence of dynamic individual psychological and collective sociocultural processes. In considering these claims, it is perhaps helpful to

---

categories to be found in these various ongoing, dynamic processes of societal-psychological construction, but that meaningful distinctions still can be made between sociocultural practices and individual psychological experience. The dynamic, emergent dualism that results from the emergence of individual psychology in sociocultural contexts is still dualism, but it is not pregiven or fixed. Rather, it is both made possible, and constrained by, mostly contingent processes of ongoing sociocultural evolution. It is into this never-ending sociocultural transformation that all biological individuals are thrown at birth, but from which, through their active participation, they may emerge as reflexive psychological agents. Because all individual psychology is necessarily emergent in this way, the dynamic ontology we have posited never can evolve into a fixed category psychological-sociocultural dualism that is typified by a categorical separation of individual psychology from sociocultural processes at individual biological birth.

14 In his extension of Vygotsky's theory of development, Harré (1984) points out that an individual can make public his or her unique transformation of an appropriated form of discourse, and in turn, have it accepted and adopted by others as a new convention or form of practice. Thus, in addition to appropriation and transformation, Harré adds sequentially two further processes he terms "publication" and "conventionalization" to indicate not only how human agents take up the practices of their culture, but further, how cultural practices can be modified and change through the contributions of individuals. In his illustration of the context of development, Harré's account shows clearly our notion of a shifting ontology of conversational and relational practices as these take their forms through the dynamic interaction between the public-social and private-individual domains.

follow Fay (1996, p. 69), and attempt to "Conceive of culture as a process of appropriation and society as a process of structuration in which meanings and rules are applied through the interpretive and willful activity of conscious agents" who "become agents only by being enculturated and socialized into a particular culture and society—processes which pre-date them, and which continue to provide the means in and through which agents can act."

At this stage, we should remind readers that the point of the foregoing positioning and elaboration of the core metaphysical and ontological thesis of dynamic interactionism is to support our claim that it is not dualism per se that has occasioned the legitimate metaphysical and epistemological concerns of textual deconstructionists, social constructionists, postmodernists, and others. Rather, such concerns are specific to the assumption of classic sociocultural-psychological dualism that societies, cultures, and selves are fixed ontological entities. Once this is recognized clearly, it is unnecessary to deny the phenomenology of human psychological experience and its possibly influential role in the kind of creativity and innovation that is required to explain the ongoing evolution and change clearly discernible in sociocultural systems. Once the emergent, mutable sociocultural and psychological ontology we have attempted to describe is in place, a defensible metaphysics is available that permits a plausible understanding of how we humans seem capable of deriving understanding from our experience that goes far beyond this experience itself. Furthermore, the kind of understanding now available makes no call on unlikely, solely mentalistic descriptions that dissipate into an unacceptable regression when put forth, as they invariably are, as explanations of exactly that which they are supposed to explain.

The key metaphysical insight is to appreciate how the sociocultural and psychological are cut from the same cloth of historical human activity (both across and within individual human lives), without either being reducible to the other. Comprehending the mutability of both individuals and societies requires an ontological recasting that moves away from the Cartesian notion of fixed sociocultural and psychological entities with set properties, to the kind of dynamic relation between sociocultural and psychological processes, conceived as relational unities, through which particular expressions of individual psychology and sociocultural systems are mutually enabled and constrained.

THE UNDERDETERMINATION THESIS

Our underdetermination thesis now can be articulated more fully and formally. We hold that personal theories, including theories of self, arise from but are underdetermined by human experience in sociocultural contexts. The theories that we hold about ourselves, others, and our circumstances originate in our lifetime experiences as participants in conversations and other sociocultural practices. However, once formed, these theories evolve in unpredictable ways that are not entirely determined by those experiences. This is because the various forms and content that we extract from our experiences are combined, edited, and revised in a never-ending, dynamic manner as material appropriated from more recent experiences interacts with that of more long-standing appropriation, as we recollect the past, anticipate and imagine the future, and act in the present. Of particular relevance to such underdetermination are ongoing modifications to our theories of self, made possible through the mediation of emergent, developing, and increasingly sophisticated memorial and imaginal capabilities.

Our minds and selves emerge gradually within the developmental context as our original existential condition of "throwness" (Heidegger, 1927/1962) unfolds and evolves. From nothing more than basic, primitive capacities to move about, perceive, and remember some of what is experienced, more differentiated and sophisticated capacities for memory (increasingly and gradually more episodic and autobiographical) and imagination (increasingly and gradually more abstracted and projective) mediate and enable a more fully dialogical sense of self as subject. Our emergent capabilities of recollecting and imagining, while developed in, and shaped by, sociocultural conversations and relations, evolve in ways that are not isomorphic with acquired conversational and conceptual forms and structures.

The fact that people become able to generate images and ideations of actual and imagined experiences constitutes an incontestable phenomenological truism. These images and ideations initially take their meanings and significance from what is appropriated and internalized from sociocultural settings. However, once emergent, the private-individual experience of episodic memories and imagined scenarios are *sui generis* psychological events. They become distinct from the meanings and significance with which they are endowed, or that we discern or interpret to be residing in them. Whatever knowledge or understanding comes of remembering and imagining experiences is not constitutive of the memory or imagined ideation per se.

The knowledge and understanding gleaned from actual and imagined experience rest on the ability to recognize kinds of things, to categorize features, and to mark them as meaningful or significant. As we develop, this ability is most often manifest as something learned rather than something remembered. In order for an experience to count as a full-fledged episodic memory, there must be reflexive consciousness of the distinction between past and present experience. We must be able to distinguish between a "me now" and a "me then." In using a learned skill, consciousness of the temporal distinction between when we first appropriated the skill and our using it now disintegrates.

For example, we commonly remark that we remember how to do certain things like read or write. However, it is uncommon for us to recollect accurately what it was like for us to be unable to read or write. In such cases, what we are doing is inferring the memory as opposed to actually experiencing it. It is only in those instances when we are able to recall an actual experience in which we learned something, or when we interpret meaning and significance in the course of examining a recollected or imagined experience, that episodic memory and learning are ostensibly connected. In such instances, our memory and imagination serve to mediate learning. On these influential occasions, our developmentally emergent capacities of episodic memory and imagination act as mediational vehicles that enable interaction between specific experiences (actual and hypothetical) and the personal theories (systems of beliefs, knowledge, skills, and attitudes) that we acquire and continuously revise through appropriating and internalizing our experiences in sociocultural settings, including our theories of self.

Our self-descriptions are refined over a lifetime of experience through a complex capacity for reflexively finding and creating meaning. In this way, experiences are woven into semicoherent autobiographies (Bruner, 1986; Taylor, 1989b). While this ever-evolving capacity for the creation of meaning is constrained by past and current sociocultural experience, it enables the creative melding of fragments of actual and imagined experience into possibilities for action. Such possibilities are generally consistent with currently emergent plans and intentions that themselves are grounded in extant personal theories. The complexity, unpredictability and inevitable imperfection (e.g., the variability of recollection in light of changing purposes and contexts) of these dynamic processes places their exact results, at any given moment, beyond our epistemic reach (in both practice and principle) as individuals and as psychologists.

Thus, our theories and actions are determined by our experiences, but are not reducible to them. Personal theories and the possibilities they contain are constrained, but underdetermined by experiential data, just as scientific theories are constrained, yet underdetermined by relevant empirical data (cf. Greenwood, 1989). However, unlike the objects of physical science, humans are reflexive, intentional construers of past, present, and future episodes and possibilities. Both the content of our personal theories, and our attempts to know them, are functions of complex indeterminate experiential histories and dynamic processes of reflexive construction that elude highly deterministic analysis. This is not to say that we can have no useful knowledge of our personal theories, including theories we hold about ourselves, or that these theories arise mysteriously. It is simply that the complexities and dynamics of socioculturally spawned personal theories, through the mediation of our emergent, reflexive capabilities of intentional remembering and imagining, make complete knowledge of our personal theories and the actions they support impossible with respect to their specific determinants. Our theories of self are constitutive of the social-public and emergent cognitive-private backgrounds from which we form our theoretical descriptions, and through which our reflexive capabilities develop. These backgrounds and capabilities defy complete articulation.

Perhaps ironically, the foregoing characteristics of personal theories and reflexivity, and their experiential underdetermination, enable human change, innovation, and creativity, even as they prevent comprehensive, deterministic understandings of them. Through our developmentally emergent, constantly evolving theories, memories, and imaginings, we humans are able to transcend our biological, experiential, sociocultural origins through creative, innovative constructions that, while constrained by these origins, are not reducible to them. This is true at both individual and collective levels of human development.

THE SHIFTING ONTOLOGY OF THE PSYCHOLOGICAL

In our account of psychological development, we have postulated developmentally emergent, increasingly sophisticated memorial and imaginal capabilities that mediate between sociocultural possibilities and constraints, and reflexive intentionality and selfhood that transcend and cannot be reduced to their biological and sociocultural origins. Prereflexive intentional consciousness is part of our embodied agency, our existentially mandated acting toward objects. Reflexive intentional consciousness is not. For human subjectivity to acquire its reflexive form, for we humans to conceive of ourselves as subjects, or selves, we must be transformed by our sociocultural experiences. This metamorphosis occurs when we take up communal conversations and practices as psychological tools with which to think dialogically and responsively. It is in this way that the psychological emerges from the sociocultural but is not reducible to it. The critical metaphysical point we wish to make in this regard is that our theory assumes a shifting, emergent ontological status for the psychological, one that develops and changes as the individual gradually develops and emerges, as reflective forms of human agency come to transcend the basic existential condition of throwness (Heidegger, 1927/1962) into preexisting physical and sociocultural worlds.

In our view, the seemingly intractable epistemological dualisms that have plagued philosophers and psychologists from the time of Descartes arise because the human mind, and other decidedly psychological entities, have been assumed to have a fixed nature. Classic and contemporary difficulties in explaining how internal mental representations of an external world might be validated have arisen from the acceptance of a fixed, unchanging ontological categorization of the mind and the physical and sociocultural world as distinct and opposed. Consequently, the philosophical search for a foundational epistemology has teetered between subjective, rational (i.e., internal) and objective, empirical (i.e., external) domains. Our conception of the psychological denies this radical dualism. We claim that, within a small number of basic biological and existential givens, the psychological is cut initially from the same cloth as the physical and sociocultural, but gradually emerges and develops beyond these origins.[15] Possibilities for human reflexive intentionality initially arise from the inevitable underdetermination of mediational

---

15 Barone, Maddux, and Snyder (1997) recently have argued that a similar type of emergent psychological ontology is evident in the work of John Dewey (1929) and George Mead (1934) (also see Dodds, Lawrence, and Valsiner, 1997). Barone et al. apply the phrase, "dual aspect theory," to this classic symbolic interactionist claim, to indicate that in these works, both social and cognitive components of human action and experience are considered to be dual aspects of a single, uniquely human symbolic, relational activity. On such an interpretation, there are clear similarities between the sociocultural-psychological metaphysics we have articulated and that of these classic forms of symbolic interactionism. However, it is important not to stretch such linkages too far. Dewey's rationalism and Mead's social behaviorism prevented them from appreciating the full psychological force of their "dual aspect" insights. Even though Dewey treated mind as distinctive, yet not discontinuous with society and physical nature, his rationalism effectively attributed to the mind powers that go beyond these "natural" conditions, as if mind stands somewhat out and above the world (see Mounce, 1997). As for Mead, his ongoing attachment to both behaviorism and innate instinctualism (see Dodds et al., 1997), restricted unduly his conception of individual psychological activity. Consequently, Mead's attempt to reconcile the social constitution of the self (Mead's "me") and the reflexive transcendence of which the self is capable (Mead's "I") ends up equating the latter with a universal collectivity–"a radically transcontextual community of interpreters" (Kögler, 1996, p. 273).

capacities for increasingly sophisticated feats of memory and imagination. However, once in place, such capacities carry the seeds of full-fledged reflexivity and selfhood, seeds that develop into reflexive forms of consciousness and awareness that enable the construction of hypothetical and projective possibilities for both individuals and the societies they inhabit. In this way, the psychological possesses a dynamic nature that grows out of, but eventually transcends, the biological, physical, and sociocultural.[16] The psychological possesses an emergent ontology, one that shifts and unfolds in the developmental context.

Our original thesis concerning the shifting ontological status of individual psychology, within the developmental context, provides a new and dynamic psychological metaphysics, one with metatheoretical implications permissive of the kind of bridging theory we have presented. From this perspective, the static, radical dualism of Descartes (1637/1960, 1641/1960) represents a profound failure to grasp the fundamental developmental truth about human psychological life—that human psychology is not pregiven, but emerges within pre-existing biological, physical, and sociocultural orders. With the emergence of genuinely reflexive capabilities associated with an evolving theory of self, psychology is made possible through the acquisition of a subject who experiences and acts in a reflective manner. The prereflective, embodied agent is transformed into a subject with reflexive intentionality, genuine autobiography, and a spatiotemporal fluidity of mind that can be exercised through heretofore unknown feats of memory and imagination.

---

16   We are reminded here of what some Anglo-American analytic philosophers refer to as the product/process fallacy (see, for example, Harré & Krausz, 1996, p. 105). "Because we agree that something has been brought into being in whole or in part by social forces does not mean that it is itself just a social fact. . . . The fact that the process by which something is brought into being has certain properties is not adequate grounds for ascribing these properties to the thing brought into being." While usually applied in arguments concerning the possible truth value of beliefs, such arguments against the product/process fallacy also serve to remind us not to conflate the origins of an entity with its emergent ontological status (contra Gergen, 1994).

3

Scientism, Relativism, and Neorealistic Hermeneutics

An Epistemology for Psychology

Much recent debate in theoretical and philosophical psychology seems to present psychologists with a Hobson's choice between scientism or relativism. Here, we attempt to explain this state of affairs, and to consider possibilities for moving between and beyond such undesirable alternatives. Ultimately, we endorse a fusion of hermeneutic and neorealist epistemologies that recognizes the uniquely dynamic, emergent ontology of psychological phenomena we have discussed herein, and which we believe is capable of warranting a progressive perspectivist program of psychological inquiry.

Throughout its 120-year history, psychology has adopted a variety of strategies (e.g., introspectionism, behaviorism, cognitivism) in an attempt to establish itself as a scientific discipline.

During this same period, numerous critics of psychology have articulated difficulties with these various strategies. Most such concerns converge on the penchant of psychologists for method and epistemology, at the expense of careful ontological and metaphysical analysis of the subject matter of psychology, particularly when that subject matter is construed as humans, their experiences, and their actions. Some critics have even accused psychologists of demonstrating embarrassing lapses of good sense in the manner in which they have conducted their affairs. Sigmund Koch (1981) has gone so far as to coin the word, "epistemopathic" (p. 258), in reference to psychologists' efforts to define psychology in terms of various inviolable methodologies and epistemologies thought to guarantee success and progress.

Such long-standing concerns have mostly been ignored by mainstream Western psychology. However, there currently are signs that this state of affairs is changing rapidly. Articles and papers scathingly critical of psychology's attempted knowledge missions, many replete with suggested correctives (qualitative, postmodern, hermeneutic, pragmatic, moral, and others), are increasingly evident in leading journals of the discipline (e.g., Bevan, 1991; Gergen, 1994; Howard, 1993; Martin, 1996; Polkinghorne, 1994; Robinson, 1991; Smith, 1994; Sugarman, 1995; Toulmin & Leary, 1994; Wertz, 1995; Williams, 1992). Sigmund Koch suddenly has a great deal of sympathy for his view that, for the most part, psychology is neither independent nor scientific (Koch, 1981).

THE SUBJECT MATTER OF PSYCHOLOGY AND THE CHALLENGES IT POSES

Ideally, any scholarly undertaking should begin with a conceptualization of its subject matter. Such consideration elevates ontological issues above epistemological considerations. While there may be no ultimate distinction between what something is thought to be and how one attempts to know it, it seems more than passing strange to apply methods of knowing in the absence of sufficiently clear conceptions of what one is attempting to know. And yet, as historians of psychology such as Danziger (1990) and Koch (1981) amply document, psychology consistently has put its epistemological/methodological cart ahead of its ontological/substantive horse.

Mostly, the favored method of achieving this peculiar end has been to follow dogmatically what psychologists have understood to be the systematic methods of physical science, on the assumption that such faithful adherence inevitably will bear the fruit of prediction and control of human behavior, if not the seeds of understanding and explanation of human experience. However, the equally dogmatic commitment displayed more recently by contemporary psychologists seemingly anxious to toil under alternate methodological yokes borrowed from fields such as computing science (e.g., Pylyshyn, 1984) and discourse analysis (e.g., Much, 1992), whatever the possible merits of such enterprises, suggests a penchant among psychologists for methodological formalism in advance of adequate conceptualization of subject matter.

Numerous scholars, past and present, have distinguished psychological phenomena from physical phenomena (Dilthey, 1894/1977; Greenwood, 1991; Kant, 1787/1965; Merleau-Ponty, 1962; Taylor, 1995). Here, following upon our previous discussion, we briefly recap three features of humans and their experiences and actions that seem central to a conceptualization of psychological subject matter, and which will serve to distinguish it from the subject matter of physical science, as well as from the focal content of scholarly undertakings that replace humans with cultural, linguistic, and other agent-absent or nonagentic systems. First, human experience and action are located in, and constituted by, both social-collective and personal-individual representations and relations (Greenwood, 1991). Experiences such as pleasure, despair, and uncertainty, and actions such as rewarding others, exacting vengeance, or striving for love and acceptance cannot be conceptualized adequately if relevant social-collective or individual-personal constituents are ignored. Such experiences and actions belong to humans and are constituted by their interpretations of the contexts they inhabit, historically and currently, and their intentions with respect to existing and future, emergent possibilities.

A second distinctive feature of psychological phenomena is the uncertainty of humans and their experiences and actions. Humans hold theories of themselves through which they are able to pursue intentionally various identity projects (cf. Harré, 1984). Such individuals are capable of creating great variation in their plans and actions based on past experiences and current perceptions and aspirations, in interaction with whatever circumstances they currently inhabit. It is inconceivable that such creativity, even if enabled and constrained by past socio-cultural experience as symbolic interactionists such as Mead (1934) and Vygotsky (1934/1986) have argued, can be determined with certainty in respect to its particulars in any specific occurrence.

Finally, a third feature of psychology's subject matter is the inevitably moral character of human action and experience, both of which are intentional in ways that reflect both choice and accountability. Whether or not one argues for this conclusion metaphysically (e.g., Kant, 1787/1965), it seems undeniable that what any of us intends to do is more than a matter of instrumental expectation determined by what we experience as needs. Intentions include desires and motives that go beyond needs, to encompass notions of what it is good to be (in character) and do (in conduct). The decisions of individuals to sacrifice their lives in the service of a cause (e.g., war) or moral dilemma (e.g., suicide) clearly illustrate this point. We humans, in our experiences and actions, are concerned with goods as goods and we act in accordance with judgments we make about the relative value of goods. We act in a practical space defined not only by what can be done and needs to be done, but by what should be done. In this way, human psychology is morally saturated.

The foregoing features of psychology's subject matter can be used to convey something of the epistemological challenges that confront psychological inquiry. The social location and individual-collective representation of psychological phenomena mean that they cannot be isolated for study in artificial, idealized settings.

When removed from their usual social and personal contexts, human experiences and actions are altered.

Without the ability to isolate and manipulate focal phenomena in ideal closed settings, we have no known method of establishing and warranting causal claims. Psychological phenomena may be causally determined, but because of their social and representative nature, and resultant susceptibility to alteration when studied scientifically, such causal relations cannot be warranted in the manner in which causal claims are established in physical science (see Martin, 1993b for a detailed elaboration of this point). The additional, highly probable possibility that psychological phenomena may be multiply determined only adds to the conclusion that the ontological status of psychological phenomena prevents their penetration by known means of establishing causal connections in physical science.

The uncertainty of psychological phenomena makes it even less likely that an adequate understanding of these phenomena will derive from the sorts of epistemological/methodological strategies employed routinely in physical science and nonagentic studies. Human experiences and actions are nested in a dynamic vortex of past experience, currently active plans and intentions, and present settings and perceptions. The creative possibilities resident in this configuration of influences clearly exceed our capacities to understand human actions and experiences with the kind of logical-mathematical specificity and certainty displayed in some branches of physical science (at least, in idealized, closed settings like some physical science laboratories) and certain formal, rule-governed environments (e.g., computational systems). This conclusion becomes even more inescapable when the moral saturation of psychological phenomena is recognized. In their practical affairs, humans are influenced not only by conceptions and understandings of what they are able to do with what possible consequences, but by what they believe it is right, proper, or good to do. The subjects of physical science are not similarly concerned (Sorell, 1991). The subject matter of psychology is thus different from the subject matter of physical science and other nonagentic subject matters, and these differences carry strong implications for epistemology and methodology in psychology.

We already have hinted strongly that much extant psychological research can, and should, be considered scientistic. We want now to explain more exactly what we mean by this claim, and to make it clear that it does not constitute an attack on science per se, nor on empirical inquiry in psychology. Further, in urging the abandonment of scientism in psychological inquiry, we have no wish to endorse a kind of relativism in which any approach, finding, or interpretation whatsoever is tenable simply because it is advocated by some individual inquirer or group of inquirers. In the same spirit as we want to distinguish scientism from legitimate science, we also will be at pains to distinguish strong relativism from a necessary perspectivism, but one that is potentially amenable to interpretive translation and critique.

Scientism in Psychological Inquiry

Broadly, we take science to be a conjunction of well-confirmed, public theories whose observational statements and theoretical postulates function to provide warranted explanations for phenomena of interest. Typically, theoretical explanations in science are warranted, at least in part, by the predictive and instrumental utility they enable in specifiable, even if constrained or idealized, situations. In psychology, theoretical explanations that display this kind of utility have been difficult to attain for reasons that relate directly to the distinctiveness of psychological phenomena. The widespread tendency of many psychologists and others to ignore such difficulties, and to persist in the belief that the methods of physical science have produced, or, given time, inevitably will produce, highly deterministic, causal understandings and explanations of humans and human actions and experiences is scientistic, not scientific.

We begin our construal of scientism by following Sorell (1991), who takes scientism to reflect "the belief that science, especially natural science, is much the most valuable part of human learning" (p. 1). Thus, the term scientism generally references the tendency to overvalue science. Almost inevitably, this overvaluing occurs at the expense of other human knowledge enterprises, such as those in the arts and humanities. This situation becomes especially acute when there are good reasons to question the appropriateness and utility of applying methods of natural (physical) science in a particular knowledge enterprise, particularly when such scientistic application can be seen to restrict and prevent forms of study and inquiry that might furnish a fuller understanding of the phenomena of interest.

We believe that psychology is this kind of knowledge enterprise, one in which the subject matter cannot reasonably be expected to yield to the same kinds of methodological and epistemological strategies that have proven successful in some branches of the natural sciences. The methods and epistemic strategies of physical science do not apply in the same way to psychological phenomena because such phenomena are morally constituted, agentically controlled, contextual, and uncertain. Progress in psychology will not be achieved if the very nature of the subject matter of psychology is overlooked, misconstrued, or ignored. If they are to be other than scientistic, advocates of physical science in psychology must present good arguments against the distinctions we have drawn between physical and psychological subject matter, and the implications for inquiry that follow from those distinctions. There may be some legitimate questions in narrow sub-areas of psychology, such as neuropsychology, where physical science may be legitimately applied in a relatively unmodified manner. However, the vast majority of psychological questions that pertain to human experience and functioning in everyday contexts requires more in the way of scholarly inquiry than the dogmatic, uncritical application of methods of understanding appropriate to physical subject matter in more restricted settings.

In making our charge of scientism, we acknowledge the possibility that much existing research in psychology, even that which is modeled after physical science, may have a certain

amount of epistemic value, even if it has not, and will not, yield
the kinds of lawful, causal understandings that are the hallmark
of success in much physical science. To the extent that empirical evidence informs legitimately contingent questions in psychological theorizing, the careful, thoughtful gathering,
consideration, and interpretation of such evidence always will
have an important place in psychological inquiry. However, relevant empirical evidence in psychology, because of the nature of
psychological phenomena, inevitably will be less generalizable,
less definitive, and more highly interpretative than the kind of
physical evidence that sometimes plays a more critical role in
the empirical testing of theories in physical science.

Relativism in Psychological Inquiry

Understandably, many psychologists whose attachment to
psychological scientism has been shaken have found solace in a
kind of psychological relativism that refuses to reject alternative
psychological theories and interpretations because they do not
square with previously favored methodological and epistemological convictions that now are known to be imperfect. Strong
relativism (what Margolis [1991] refers to as relationalism or
relational relativism) holds that what is true is relative to a
conceptual scheme, and that what is true in one such scheme,
and for its possessor, will be false for another. Weak relativism
(what Margolis refers to as robust relativism) is a more constrained antidote for dogmatism in which what it is reasonable
to believe is relative to a conceptual scheme, and what it is
reasonable to believe in one conceptual scheme may not be reasonable to believe in another. The distinction between strong
and weak relativism (following Appiah [1989] and Margolis) plays
a great deal on the distinction between truth and belief. While
there may be a single reality, particularly in the physical world
we inhabit, our knowledge of it always is, of necessity, conceptually or theoretically framed, and what we take as reasonable to
believe will be determined, at least in part, by such conceptual
frameworks. In holding to weak relativism, one is not committed to anything more than this. In strong relativism, one is com-

mitting oneself to the view that reality and truth are relative to differing conceptual schemes. If this latter is so, the possibility of understanding, even of communication, across conceptual frameworks is impossible, a thesis that Kuhn (1970) and others have referred to as incommensurability. The weaker form of relativism is not linked to this kind of incommensurability, but holds that cross-framework communication and understanding is possible, if difficult and problematic.[17]

Perhaps the most powerful logical argument against strong relativism is that its epistemological incommensurability with respect to truth claims is incoherent because to claim that truth itself is relative leads to the conclusion that there will be as many truths as there are conceptual schemes. And, more tellingly, that what is true in one scheme will be false in another. Thus, strong relativism amounts to saying that what is true is false, and vice versa without end. For this reason, few scholars are willing to commit themselves to strong relativism. Weak relativism is, however, another matter. In holding that beliefs are relative to conceptual schemes, one is not committed to "true-false" incompatibilities across schemes. Further, for weak relativists it may be the case that some beliefs are more or less well-supported, logically and empirically, both within and across conceptual schemes.

An important formal criticism of all relativism (Newton-Smith, 1981) is that rival conceptual schemes and the epistemological claims they support cannot be incompatible if the meanings of their terms are different. Under strict incommensurability this must be so, because if a particular key term appears in different, rival schemes, it is necessarily embedded in different

---

17   Our discussion of relativism is necessarily simplified. In focusing on two general kinds of epistemic relativism (i.e., strong and weak), we purposefully are not attempting to draw out all the varieties of epistemic relativism that have been proposed. We also are limiting our discussion by not addressing ontological, semantic, and moral relativisms. The interested reader might wish to consult Harré and Krausz (1996) for a comprehensive consideration of the wide varieties of relativism available in contemporary philosophy.

webs of meaning. Thus, if the term means different things in different schemes, there is nothing necessarily incompatible in employing the term within and across different conceptual schemes. As already argued, with respect to weak relativism, beliefs may lack meaning, and be difficult to understand when viewed outside of a particular scheme, but they will not be incompatible across schemes because their meanings will differ. If there is no necessary incompatibility, there is no basis for saying that epistemological claims constituted of such terms are relative, in the sense of incompatible. A particular form of weak relativism, what we call perspectivism, actually takes advantage of logical considerations of this kind, and, we believe, has special relevance for psychology, given the nature of psychological subject matter.

Perspectivism may be particularly attractive to psychologists who wish to avoid both scientistic dogmatism and the epistemological consequences of strong relativism. In perspectivism, the epistemological claims of different conceptual schemes are viewed as offering possible interpretations of a focal phenomena, views that are different, not necessarily incompatible, and potentially subject to adjudication and possible reconciliation. Examples of different descriptions of psychological phenomena offered from different conceptual schemes might include, "Susan is upset," "Susan's spirit is broken," "Susan is engaging in negative self-talk," and so forth. These claims inevitably are associated with different explanations for Susan's experience and actions. Because perspectivism does not assume that such interpretations are necessarily incompatible, psychological inquiry is free to attempt to understand the meanings and functions of these various understandings both within and across the various conceptual schemes that contain them. The ultimate aim of such inquiry is to forge a more adequate conceptualization, understanding, and explanation of humans and human action and experience than might be forthcoming if psychological inquiry is more conceptually restricted.

Perspectivism does not eschew reasons and evidence as essential warrants for understanding, nor is it committed to finding that all conceptual schemes are equally valuable. It is a weak relativism that holds that our concepts are partly constitutive of the reality about which we offer reasons and evidence. However, by not endorsing the true-false incompatibility of strong relativism, perspectivism holds out the promise of bridging different understandings from different conceptual schemes through the forging of newly emergent conceptual schemes—a possible result of dynamic interactions between processes of inquiry and existing, evolving frameworks of understanding and purpose (e.g., Gadamer, 1960/1975). Exactly how such emergent understandings are to be justified and supported by evidence and reason currently is not well established across various perspectivist proposals, although several specific suggestions and illustrations are available (see Hoshmand & Martin, 1995). For our current purposes, it is sufficient to note that the possibility of such warrants of justification is consistent with our notion of perspectivism in psychological inquiry. Later, we will argue that in order to be progressive with respect to warranting advances in psychological knowledge, perspectivism is best considered in ways consistent with an elaborated version of Gadamer's philosophical hermeneutics.

No discussion of relativism in psychology should ignore the fact that much of the subject matter of psychology, together with our ways of studying this subject matter, are artifacts of human construction. One common way of referring to this state of affairs is to say that psychology is doubly interpretative, in contrast to physical science, which most (aside from a very few strong physical relativists) see as singly interpretative in its manner of study only. It seems undeniable that, outside of certain biological constraints, we humans through our actions and experiences are both products, and producers, of social and psychological practices.

Yet, to adopt strongly relativistic approaches to psychological inquiry seems to deny the possibility that there are, on the one hand, undeniable aspects of human experience that spring from the very nature of our existence in the world, and, on the other hand, ways of communicating across the sociocultural, linguistic, interpersonal, and personal conventions and practices that separate us. If taken to its logical extreme, such relativism would seem to deny the possibility of psychology itself, reducing human experience to nothing more than entirely local, individual occurrences and fleeting impressions that resist generalization, understanding, and explanation.

On this construal there would exist no bases whatsoever for judging certain human experiences and actions as more or less useful, valuable, appropriate, or sensible, because any bases for rendering such judgments would be eroded by unfettered incompatibilism. It is difficult to conceive of any intellectual or scholarly enterprise, psychological or not, that could exist, let alone flourish, under such a view. With very few exceptions, even those most staunchly and consistently critical of psychology's scientistic tendencies have no desire to bury psychological inquiry under this kind of relativism. In Koch's (1993) words, we "all are responding however idiosyncratically or tendentiously—or speculatively, or empirically, or practically—to a challenge endemic to the human condition: namely, to understand it in ever-increasing depth and salience, perhaps to enrich and even ennoble that condition" (p. 902).

A NEOREALIST HERMENEUTICS

If the ontological status of psychological phenomena is as interrelational, emergent, evolving, and mutable as the kind of sociocultural-psychological interactionism we have described (see ch. 2 above) asserts, what kind of epistemology will suffice for claiming and justifying knowledge of psychological phenomena in terms of the relations, constraints, and possibilities that define them? Our answer to this complex question consists of two interacting strategic components. The first follows from an appreciation of the impermanent, yet nonetheless real nature of both sociocultural and psychological phenomena, and consists of the empirical demonstration of possibilities and constraints that psychological theories somehow must acknowledge. The second component in our epistemic proposal concerns the critical evaluation of different theoretical formulations intended to account for the empirically demonstrated possibilities and constraints.

Because there is no definitive way of ascertaining the true fit between theoretical formulations and focal psychological phenomena, it always is possible to formulate different viable theories reflecting different interpretations of the demonstrations in question. Consequently, the evaluation of competing theories, and the means and criteria of any such evaluation, must be considered not only in relation to relevant demonstrations themselves, but also in relation to the traditions of understanding and knowing in which both demonstrations and theories are embedded. This evaluation inevitably involves the translation and critique of the competing theories and perspectives in terms of each other and their supporting traditions. In what follows, we will discuss each component of our epistemological strategy in turn, and then attempt to show why it is particularly well suited to the provision and warranting of knowledge claims concerning the dynamic, interactionist sociocultural–psychological metaphysics and ontology we have discussed earlier.

Demonstrations and Theories of Possibilities and Constraints
Because sociocultural and psychological phenomena are the dynamically evolving artifacts of collective and individual human activity, their ontological status differs from that of physical phenomena. Since human inquiry into these constructions is itself a set of human practices, the study of sociocultural and psychological phenomena is doubly interpretive in a manner foreign to the study of physical phenomena. However, the actively constructed, constantly evolving nature of human phenomena only means that such phenomena are impermanent. It does not mean that they are not real. Most importantly, the ontological status of these phenomena does not suggest that they can be interpreted in any manner whatsoever. Our conceptions of sociocultural and psychological phenomena, as well as these phenomena themselves, are grounded in social, cultural, linguistic,

and historical conventions. As products of these dynamic processes, they are not so ephemeral as to escape attempts to scrutinize them. Sociocultural and psychological phenomena are real in the sense that they both enable and constrain themselves and our interpretations of them. Such influence, while never static, cannot be dismissed.

For example, it certainly is not the case that we could, without extensive sociocultural engineering of the most unlikely sort, construct and use different conceptual models for psychological phenomena such as aggressiveness and hostility in our theories of such phenomena in contemporary Western societies. Within a particular sociocultural tradition, our descriptions and interpretations of human actions and social practices are linguistically objective because their accuracy, appropriateness, or correctness can be adjudicated according to whether the phenomena concerned have the properties attributed to them by our descriptions and interpretations. Thus, the labeling of an action as aggressive is warranted only if it is represented by the agent in question as harmfully directed toward another. This is because of the intentional nature of such labels. On the other hand, actions may be described accurately as hostile if and only if the forms of behavior involved are conventionally represented by members of a sociocultural collective as inimical to an other. This latter determination is linguistically independent of the specific intentions of the agent. Such linguistic conventions and the sociocultural traditions that support them form a kind of reality against which we can examine the adequacy and utility of our descriptions and interpretations (Greenwood, 1991). The precise nature of this impermanent, humanly constructed reality is that it both enables and constrains human interpretive practices, including the inquiry practices of social scientists and psychologists.

Because sociocultural and psychological phenomena are dynamic and relational in time and space, the properties, processes, and functions they comprise never can be determined in any definitive, timeless, or context-free manner. Our theories of them cannot be based on definitive tests that establish or refute specific claims resident in our theories. However, we can base our interpretations and theories of sociocultural and psychological phenomena on our interpretations of empirical demonstrations of the kinds of constraints and possibilities they exert and enable. As real, although impermanent processes, such phenomena are capable of exerting considerable influence.

Of course, all psychological theories are empirical in that human experience in the pre-existing and evolving physical and sociocultural world provides the basis for all of our beliefs. However, this kind of necessary, inevitable grounding of our beliefs is insufficient for warranting our theories of psychological phenomena. Knowledge goes beyond experience in that, while certainly not static nor universally or eternally true, it must meet, or take explicitly account of, relevant public standards of meaning and evidence, as these have been (and are) constructed, and subscribed to, by communities of individuals active in the study of these phenomena. In short, psychological theories require experience, but experience alone is not a sufficient basis for theoretical development in social science and psychology.

Theories in psychology develop through a complex, public articulation of psychologists' understanding of human experience made possible by an ongoing immersion and participation in social life in general, and in the forms and content of understanding and knowing that constitute social science and psychology. Empirical investigations intended to support and/or refute important aspects of these theories might best be thought of as demonstrations of the possibilities and constraints enabled and exerted by the focal phenomena. Such demonstrations become increasingly useful for the purposes of theory construction and revision as the theories themselves are elaborated and refined in an ongoing, repetitive cycle of dynamic interpretation and reassessment in relation to relevant demonstrations. Understood in this way, much extant inquiry in social science and psychology (at least, that which does not conceptualize and reduce its subject matter inappropriately) can be stripped of its unsupportable vestiges of objectivism and positivism, and seen as a valuable source of necessarily socioculturally and temporally constrained demonstrations of what is possible and influential in human practices, actions, and experiences. This more fallibilist construal of social and psychological inquiry assumes that its focal phenomena are impermanent, yet real, and cannot be construed in manners unsupported by relevant sociocultural traditions, including those that define the inquiry practices of psychologists and social scientists.

Translations and Critical Fusions

But, what happens when different inquirers, with memberships in different traditions, offer competing accounts of psychological and sociocultural phenomena from the perspectives of the traditions in which they are immersed? Because demonstrations of theoretical possibilities and constraints are themselves necessarily embedded in particular sociocultural traditions and practices of inquiry, is one then required to conclude, even while acknowledging that within such traditions and practices it is not the case that "anything goes," that there is no way of moving beyond the impasse created by the possibility of different theories from different traditions and perspectives? In other words, while strong relativism is clearly overcome within traditions of inquiry, does it nonetheless hold sway across different traditions of inquiry and their epistemic products?

Sociocultural-psychological dynamic interactionism takes an ontological position of emergent, dynamic psychological realism, the etiology of which is located mostly in real sociocultural practices that also are subject to ongoing change. This ontology seems most compatible with the kind of philosophical hermeneutics articulated by Gadamer (1975, 1977). Gadamer's epistemological position avoids the radical relativism sometimes associated with postmodern textualism (e.g., Derrida, 1978), and provides a solid, identifiable basis for the kind of epistemic pragmatism associated with much social constructionist thought (Gergen, 1991, 1994). Furthermore, we believe it can be adapted to do this without conflating emergent psychological phenomena with their mostly sociocultural origins. Simply creating a different narrative is not epistemically satisfactory unless this narrative adheres to, and achieves coherence within, the relevant sociocultural reality. All human understanding and knowledge are perspectival, but in relation to real sociocultural traditions (here, both we and Gadamer follow Heidegger, 1949, 1927/1962). Interpretations of social collectives or of psychological individuals that fall outside of, or defy constraints imposed by, relevant traditions fail to impress.

There is no way of escaping from the sociocultural traditions in which societies and psychological individuals are embedded. There is no outside vantage point, complete with its own set of unimpeachably objective standards, from which to make judgments concerning the relative merits of different interpretations. This is especially true when the subject matter of the interpretations being considered consists of human sociocultural and/or psychological phenomena. When interpretations differ legitimately, it is because they are drawn from different sociocultural and psychological traditions. Gadamer's metaphor for moving beyond the impasse in interpretive understanding that seemingly follows from such difference is "a fusion of horizons." Gadamer rejects the radical incommensurability between competing traditions, and posits the possibility of fusions across them. These fusions result from honest attempts to understand different interpretations and the traditions supporting them. When such attempts ("conversations") are legitimate, joined seriously, and sustained, the resultant fusions are inevitable and differ from any of the competing traditions in their substantive claims and warrants of justification.

Because the possibility of illegitimate interpretations exists (i.e., interpretations not appropriately constrained by any identifiable tradition), participants in these conversations always retain the right to disagree, once such illegitimate impasses are recognized (see Warnke, 1987). Gadamerian hermeneutics thus assumes that sociocultural traditions are real and must be treated seriously in attempts to form and defend interpretations of sociocultural and psychological phenomena. Because such phenomena are constituted historically and are contingent, relevant traditions are the only feasible epistemic source available to scholars in the humanities and social sciences.

Of course, Gadamer's insistence on the inescapability and utility of sociocultural traditions as a basis for the avoidance of strong relativism through his construct of fusions, has been hotly contested by contemporary critical hermeneuts (e.g., Habermas, 1971, 1984) and postmodernists (e.g., Lyotard, 1987). In recognition of the difficulties that might be encountered in adjudicating when attempts at cross-tradition, interpretive translation ("conversation") possess legitimate good faith and when they do not, Habermas has insisted it is necessary to articulate some kind of universal pragmatics that defines communicative competence, thus forming a kind of metahermeneutics that serves as a discursive bridge across different interpretations and the traditions in which they are embedded. In a different direction, Lyotard objects strenuously to Gadamer's relatively conservative appeal to established traditions of interpretation, arguing that such attachment furthers the essentially unwarranted prejudices of powerful, vested interests of traditional groups of knowledge makers.

In response, Gadamer insists on the possibility of laying claim to both rational and moral argument without standing outside of historical traditions of understanding and inquiry. He holds that these traditions are the only possible bases for deciding between competing interpretive and theoretical accounts, and that the ever-present possibility of fusion undermines the conservativism that otherwise might attend such a reliance on traditions. On this view, attempts, like that of Habermas, to step outside competing and available traditions to forge an independent basis for warranting are impossible. Furthermore, attempts, like that of Lyotard, to radically reconstruct the status quo, are inevitably regressive, nihilistic, and egocentric, because they court both unintelligibility and unbridled self-interest in their suggestions that knowledge projects are conceivable outside of historical, sociocultural traditions and their fusions.

The kind of dynamic sociocultural-psychological metaphysics we discussed earlier in this book shares with Gadamer's hermeneutics, an emphasis on the real, yet shifting, nature of sociocultural traditions. Because of the way in which it conceives of the psychological as derivative from, but not reducible to, the sociocultural, this kind of dynamic interactionism also is amenable to the view that epistemological claims concerning psychological phenomena can only be adjudicated in relation to relevant sociocultural traditions and their fusions. All potentially creative, innovative contributions of psychological individuals, including communities of inquirers in psychology and social science, must meet and surpass warrants of justification available in relevant sociocultural traditions and their fusions. In this way, necessary distinctions between beliefs (of psychological individuals) and knowledge (socioculturally sanctioned claims and warrants through which beliefs and understandings of psychological individuals can be assessed) are maintained, and intelligibility is preserved within a dynamic, ever-emergent epistemological process that accompanies the dynamic interactive metaphysical context charted earlier. The possibility that the beliefs and actions of psychological individuals, including psychologists, may advance relevant sociocultural, shared knowledge, and be judged to do so on the basis of traditional warrants, and/or extensions to same (as a result of legitimate fusions) serves as a viable basis for epistemic justification. In this way, a middle course is charted between the extremes of an overly constraining static, ahistorical, "outside" standard on the one bank, and an overly enabling, strongly relativistic, nihilistic, "anything goes" absence of standard on the other.[18]

---

18   While Gadamer, following Heidegger, presented his philosophical hermeneutics as an alternative to classical approaches to metaphysics and the separation of ontology and epistemology, we are unapologetic in claiming philosophical hermeneutics as an epistemological strategy that fits with our metaphysical arguments in support of dynamic interactionism. Gadamer's rejection of metaphysics and epistemology was based on an understanding of metaphysics and ontology as concerned primarily with the positing of universal, fixed categories that could serve as a firm foundation for epistemological certainty. However, as we already have argued, we reject this absolutist approach to metaphysics, ontology, and epistemology. Saying things exist and have a nature need not necessarily imply that their existence and nature are fixed or universal. Our central metaphysical claim concerning

A key ingredient to all of this is, of course, a sufficiently powerful notion of what constitutes legitimate good faith in the translation and critical consideration of competing interpretations and theories. Once objectivism and positivism are abandoned in favor of a fallibilist, perspectivist epistemology, some powerful, coherent notion of "critical intersubjectivity" is required to enable the necessarily imperfect (but all that is available) possibility of Gadamer's fusion of horizons.

Critical Intersubjectivity

The kind of perspectivism advanced by Gadamer, and subscribed to above, entails a critical recognition that no psychological inquiry possibly can yield singular, objective truths that correspond directly to a fixed sociocultural/psychological reality. Instead, the only kind of objectivity that is possible is one of critical intersubjectivity that might be achieved through fair-minded criticism and accountability both within and across traditions of understanding and inquiry. When various investigators working within the same and different traditions of inquiry

---

psychological and sociocultural phenomena is that their existence and nature are dynamic and emergent, but no less real or epistemically influential for all of that. Thus, when Gadamer (1975) argues that our psychological consciousness is effected historically, we understand him to make a fundamental point about the necessarily hermeneutical character of our experience of the world, one that puts a kind of ongoing interpretive emergence from our profoundly sociocultural participations at the very heart of our human nature. It is this dynamic, interpretive flow that is the universal basis for our nature as psychological individuals, whatever the necessarily contingent arrangements of our psychologies might be in any particular times and contexts.

Most important for our epistemic purposes is Gadamer's depiction of understanding as participation in an occurrence of tradition. This means that our emergent subjectivity is not the appropriate basis for determining sense from nonsense. Our psychological being, as historically effected consciousness, is more substance than subjectivity. Our understanding is the continuation of a sociocultural dialogue into which we are thrown, and which we carry on. In each new encounter, we take over and modify what

conduct demonstrations that they interpret as supportive of their theoretical formulations, they also must engage in an ongoing dialogue with rival inquirers. In this dialogue, inquirers must attempt sincerely and openly to understand the theories and interpretations of others through the construction of translations and fusions that open into the possibility that rival views may have merits that surpass their own. This involves the systematic examination of one's own and rival views in a careful, critically probing, and fair-minded manner. This kind of critical intersubjectivity features co-operative, collective conversations bent on discerning the worth of rival theories, modes of inquiry, and systems of justification.

It is important to note that none of this demands that investigators abandon their preconceptions and attempt to attain an entirely detached, outside view of the matters under consideration. As Gadamer has argued, no such outside vantage point is possible or necessary. What is necessary is that critical intersubjectivity be exercised so that the outcomes of programs

---

makes sense in terms of the traditions presented to, and present in, us. Our understanding is not in the form of isolated consciousness, but in terms of hermeneutic dialogue realized in the dialectic of question and answer. Only in conversation that displays good faith in confrontation with another's thought (and its traditions) can we go beyond the limits of our present horizon of understanding.

And yet, Gadamer (1975) also argues that becoming conscious of being historically, socioculturally effected is a task always to be undertaken. One's hermeneutic situation calls for a critical awareness of the presuppositions, prejudices, and limitations of one's situated understanding. Thus, Gadamer advocates the self-interpretation of facticity and the critical recognition of finitude that inevitably attend the human condition. "The possibility that the other person may be right is the soul of hermeneutics" (Gadamer, July 9, 1989, as cited in Grondin, 1994, p. 124). In all of this, Gadamer's philosophical hermeneutics assumes a socioculturally situated, emergent self in constant communion with others. It is a self that comes to possess a critical, interpretive reflexivity that originates in, yet goes beyond, its situation, even while being simultaneously constrained by its situatedness.

of inquiry are not determined by the inevitable preconceptions and biases of particular investigators or groups of investigators.[19]

All researchers work within traditions of discourse that provide them with necessary tools and conceptual resources with which to conduct their inquiries. But, traditions are not closed, fixed and immune from internal and external criticism. Critical intersubjectivity requires that researchers both (a) acknowledge necessary and inevitable contingent limits on their theoretical and methodological practices and the ontological and epistemological assumptions that support them, and (b) take seriously and respond constructively to fair-minded criticisms of their practices and assumptions. This means that they must examine critically their basic conceptual commitments, their conceptions of evidence, their standards of significance, and take into consideration the manner in which their investigations are positioned socially and morally (see, e.g., Fay, 1996; Hoshmand & Martin; 1995; Martin, 1996). It also means that inquirers must be accountable for their intellectual and evaluative commitments, and "acknowledge their positionality vis-à-vis other investigators, their audiences, and those under study" (Fay, 1996, p. 219).

In summary, the main epistemological ideas advanced above include (a) a conception of inquiry practice in terms of necessarily imperfect, revisable theoretical formulations in constant interac-

---

19 Some critical hermeneuts (e.g., Kögler, 1996) argue that Gadamer's philosophical hermeneutics must be extended to guard against the possibility that "other" accounts will be too readily assimilated into a theorist's favored position. To ensure that dialogue across theoretical perspectives is sufficiently open and critical, they suggest that theorists must actually distance themselves actively from their own theories during such discourse. By actively privileging the alternatives available in other theoretical perspectives, this purposeful self-distanciation enables a perception of one's own perspective as more foreign and problematic than it otherwise has been seen to be. With this kind of dialogical self-distanciation in place, the likelihood that resultant fusion will prematurely assimilate differences necessary for critical reflection is greatly reduced. What we want to take from Gadamer is consistent with this critical strategy, and is one of the reasons why we refer to our reading and use of Gadamer's ideas as neo-Gadamerian or neorealist hermeneutics.

tion with interpretations of relevant empirical demonstrations; (b) the explicit recognition that all such practices are conducted within traditions that support the assumptions, biases, theories, interpretations, and investigative strategies and methodologies of researchers; and (c) the possibility of fusions, which can result from the engagement of critical intersubjectivity, and which might advance understanding and knowledge about focal phenomena both within and across traditions of inquiry. This dynamic, perspectivist, and fallibilist epistemology might be thought of as a kind of neorealist hermeneutics that accepts the ontological status of sociocultural and psychological phenomena as real, yet impermanent and emergent, processes that are constantly evolving and mutating as a consequence of their dynamic interaction. The important epistemological point is that all of this dynamic change occurs within existing sociocultural and psychological processes and traditions that, while impermanent, both make possible and constrain their own evolution. This is what permits psychologists and other social scientists to inquire into sociocultural and psychological phenomena and achieve knowledge that, while contingent, perspectival, and fallible, is nonetheless useful within and across the boundaries of traditions of inquiry and knowledge practices.

Our Thesis in Summary

Thus far, we have attempted to elaborate a theory of how individual psychological phenomena originate in, emerge from, and develop within sociocultural forms and practices, but do not reduce to these sociocultural means. In the previous part of our book, we attempted an ontological clarification of what we termed dynamic sociocultural-psychological interactionism, distinguishing it from classic sociocultural-psychological dualism and from postmodern textualism and social constructionism. In so doing, we also attempted to position this processural interactionism in relation to recent suggestions for moving beyond debates between atomists and holists in contemporary philosophy of social science, and social constructionists and cognitive constructivists in psychology. In this chapter of our book, we have attempted to articulate and defend an epistemological position compatible with the dynamic interactionist sociocultural-psychological metaphysics and ontology we discussed earlier. We termed this epistemological position neorealist hermeneutics, and attempted to describe it as an approach to attaining and warranting knowledge of psychological and sociocultural phenomena through psychological and social scientific inquiry—which we understand as an ongoing interaction of theoretical formulation and empirical demonstration within and across different traditions of inquiry practice and their fusions, with particular emphasis on a kind of neo-Gadamerian critical intersubjectivity as a defining characteristic.

If we have succeeded in our aims, it should now be possible to glimpse clearly, if not completely, two important possibilities with respect to the forging of a more satisfactory philosophical basis (both ontologically and epistemologically) for psychological inquiry than that afforded by classic sociocultural-psychological dualism and either traditional objectivism or postmodern relativism. The first possibility is that of defending a viable ontological position for psychological phenomena that does not flounder on the rocks of classic, fixed entity dualism, but which preserves nonmysterious distinctions between emergent psychological phenomena and the sociocultural contexts that spawn them. The second possibility is that of defending a workable epistemology that is compatible with this ontological position and which avoids both the scientism involved in applying objectivist, positivist, physical scientific methodologies and epistemologies to psychological phenomena without regard to the agentic, contextualized nature of such phenomena, and the strong relativism that seems too often to accompany the necessary endorsement of perspectivism and fallibilism in psychology and social science. In short, if our aims have been met, readers now should be in a position to envision psychological inquiry as nested ontologically between classic dualism and antipsychological reductionism (such as postmodern textualism, social constructionism, and eliminative materialism), and epistemologically between scientism and strong relativism.

Such a psychology is both made possible and constrained by the same sociocultural traditions and fusions that enable and constrain the emergence and development of psychological phenomena themselves. Both sociocultural traditions and the collective and individual psychologies embedded within them are contingent, perspectival, and fallible, yet nonetheless real. Our neorealist hermeneutics embraces the possibilities of interpretive translation and critical intersubjectivity as means of avoiding strong relativism and incommensurability across different sociocultural traditions and psychological perspectives. When these metaphysical and epistemological views are applied to our own practices of inquiry, we psychologists emerge as psychological individuals embedded in our societies and cultures, including our traditions of inquiry practice, but with the possibility of transcending the current forms of these practices and the knowledge claims and warrants they contain. Such transcendence is made possible by virtue of our agentic intentionality and capacity for critical reflexivity (both subjective and intersubjective), when these are targeted at a deeper understanding of our own nature and the conditions of constraint and possibility that warrant our necessarily imperfect knowledge of it.

4

Applying A Psychology of Possibility and Constraint

Psychotherapy

As described in Chapter 2, our theory of psychological development is an attempt to explain how human action and experience undergo and display change, learning, and innovation. We envision an ongoing, dynamic process simultaneously constrained by sociocultural participation and experience, and made possible by emergent and developing capabilities for reflexive forms of memory and imagination. These reflexive capacities, because of their underdetermination by their largely sociocultural origins and because of their spatiotemporal fluidity, enable a transcendence beyond the participations and experiences of the present and the past. They create a kind of individual psychology nonexistent and unknown in their absence, one that is reflexively organized around an emergent and evolving theory of self. In so doing, they shift the very ontological status of human psychology within the developmental context. In framing and articulating this theory, we have assumed nothing more than primitive biological capacities to move about in pre-existing physical and sociocultural worlds and to perceive and remember something of the embodied experience that inevitably unfolds as a consequence of this basic existential situation.

We believe that the most important metaphysical aspect of our work is to be found in our rejection of fixed category dualism combined with our insistence that psychological phenomena, once emergent, are not reducible to their largely sociocultural origins. We have insisted that human innovation and change, and the general capacity to go beyond past experience and accomplishment are not mysterious or inexplicable. Yet, we also have insisted that these creative possibilities cannot be reduced to tight determinisms that essentially deny these very same accomplishments. Our compromise is a form of dynamic relational, emergent dualism in which psychological development, change, and innovation are seen as products of our functional engagement with the pre-existing physical and sociocultural worlds into which we are thrown, but by which we ultimately are not entirely constrained because of our emergent capacities for memory, imagination, and selfhood. These capacities exist in a state of constant, dynamic flux that carries the seeds of human creativity and change.

Our original thesis concerning the shifting ontological status of individual psychology, within the developmental context we have described, provides a new and dynamic psychological metaphysics, one with metatheoretical implications permissive of the kind of bridging theory we have presented. From this perspective, the static, radical dualism of Descartes (1637/1960, 1641/1960) represents a profound failure to grasp the fundamental developmental truth about human psychological life—that human psychology is not pregiven, but emerges within pre-existing biological, physical, and sociocultural orders. With the emergence of genuinely reflexive capabilities associated with an evolving theory of self, individual psychology is made possible through the acquisition of a subject who experiences and acts in a reflective manner. Merleau-Ponty's (1962) prereflective embodied agent is transformed into a subject with reflexive intentionality, genuine autobiography, and a spatiotemporal fluidity of mind that can be exercised through heretofore unknown feats of memory and imagination.

What we want to do in this and the next chapter of our book is to explain and demonstrate how our theory of human psychological development plays out in practical understanding, and in particular, enables an enhanced understanding of psychotherapy, education, and human creativity and innovation. In each of these areas, we will examine current controversies and debates between sociocultural and cognitive-constructivistic positions. We also will elaborate and instantiate our own theory into these debates and discussions, and attempt to articulate what we consider to be the advantages and advances in understanding that result. Our primary concern is to illustrate some of the ways in which our theoretical perspective prepares us to think differently, and we believe more productively, about some of those institutions and practices in contemporary Western society that are most concerned with the promotion of human development, learning, change, and innovation. At times, the kind of enhanced understanding we advocate, and attempt to convey, involves reconceptualizing more traditional and common views and assumptions. At other times, our views incorporate and extend what we consider to be the most promising of previous work in those fields to which we now turn.

SOCIAL CONSTRUCTIONIST AND COGNITIVE CONSTRUCTIVIST PERSPECTIVES ON PSYCHOTHERAPY

For the most part, theories of psychotherapeutic practice have emphasized conceptual foundations more similar to those held by cognitive constructivists than to those promoted by social constructionists. Given that psychotherapy attempts to induce change in clients' ways of experiencing, living, problem-solving, and coping, it makes sense that psychotherapeutic theories of practice tend to focus on the capacities of individuals for change, coping, and resolution of their problems and difficulties. This emphasis on individualistic forms of change and development also is consistent with the standard form of psychotherapy as practiced in Western cultures, consisting primarily of conversational interaction between an individual psychotherapist and an individual client. For example, one of the first forms of psychotherapy to be widely practiced was that developed by Sigmund Freud (1914/1966). While certainly concerned with happenings in clients' life experiences outside of the therapeutic hour, Freud devoted most of his theory and practice to the uncovering of supposedly repressed memories, the reenactment and reexperiencing of events symbolized in those memories, and the apparently resultant resolution of clients' dysfunctional symptoms and lifestyles.

Only during the 1920s to the 1960s was psychotherapy cast as a process of social construction, and then only by a minority of theorists and practitioners of psychotherapy who identified with very narrow, reductionistic versions of behavioral psychology. For the most part, these approaches to psychology and to psychotherapy bore little resemblance to the kind of social constructionist thinking described and discussed in this volume. Where the behaviorists were concerned primarily with habitual forms of experiencing, thinking, and acting, supposedly tied directly to specific environmental triggers, true social constructionism suggests that knowledge does not reside exclusively either in the minds of individuals or in the environment but rather in the social processes of symbolic interaction and exchange.

More recently, there are indications that more bona fide forms of social constructionist thought are beginning to find their way into the thinking and theorizing of some scholars and practitioners of psychotherapy. This is most notable in the work of Gergen (Gergen & Gergen, 1991; McNamee & Gergen, 1992) and others who have advocated a postmodern variant of social constructionism that

> draws attention to the manner in which conventions of language and other social processes (negotiation, persuasion,

power, etc.) influence the accounts rendered of the "objective" world. The emphasis is thus not on the individual mind but on the meanings of people as they collectively generate descriptions and explanations in language. (Gergen & Gergen, 1991, p. 78)

Such postmodern forms of social constructionism (also see Lather, 1992; Sampson, 1983) move away from traditional emphases of psychotherapy theorists on the individual self, sometimes going so far as to talk about the death of the self, implying a dissolution of any conception of individuality as a unitary entity distinguishable from activity within the sociocultural milieu. Such deconstructionist scholarship celebrates the demise of the sovereign individual and its replacement by more anonymous forms of ongoing social exchange. As Sass (1992) observes,

Instead of the old pathos of distance . . . the condition of an inner self cut off from some unattainable reality—we enter into a universe devoid of both objects and selves: where there is only a swarming of "selfobjects," images and simulacra filling us without resistance. (p. 176)

However, as already noted, the presence of truly social constructionist, self-less psychologies is mostly absent in the area of psychotherapy theory and practice. Perhaps more so than any other area of applied psychology, psychotherapeutic theories of practice have tended to embrace cognitive constructivist views. Clearly, such perspectives are naturally friendly to the institution of Western psychotherapy. Following Neimeyer (1995), most extensions of constructivistic thought in the area of psychotherapy may be subsumed under five basic metaphors: (a) therapy as personal science, (b) therapy as the development of self, (c) therapy as conceptual revision, (d) therapy as a kind of narrative reconstruction, and (e) therapy as conversational elaboration. For the most part, mainstream cognitive and cognitive-behavioral psychologies, including contemporary work in the area of social cognition and cognitive development, have contributed heavily to notions of therapy as self-development and as reconstruction of personal schemas or conceptual frameworks.

The metaphor of *therapy as personal science* involves viewing the client in psychotherapy as a scientist actively formulating and testing personal hypotheses, and adjusting systems of personal hypotheses and theories in light of experiential tests and feedback. This, of course, is the fundamental proposal of George Kelly's (1955) personal construct psychology. Psychotherapy theorists like Epting (1984), Neimeyer and Neimeyer (1987), and many others have developed extensive models of psychotherapy based on this central idea. However, the metaphor of therapy as personal science also has been attractive to many cognitively oriented psychotherapists who have interpreted the notion of personal science in traditional logical, empiricist ways, maintaining only a semblance of Kelly's brand of constructivism (e.g., Meichenbaum [1977] who incorporates some of Vygotsky's work into a generally cognitive-constructivistic view of psychotherapy and psychotherapeutic change).

Therapy as the development of self harkens back to very early forms of psychoanalytic theorizing about the acquisition of early maladaptive schemas thought to underlie serious psychological disturbance. Currently, many scholars of psychotherapy have begun to focus again on early developmental stages (Freeman, 1993) or attachment relationships (Bricker, Young, & Flannigan, 1993) in which various disordered self-schemas are thought to arise, a terrain once exclusively the property of psychodynamic therapists.

At least two influential theorists, Guidano (1987, 1991) and Liotti (1986), have combined the therapeutic metaphor of self-development with that of personal science. Liotti (1986) explicitly models his conceptualization of the structure of self and other personal theories after the structure of scientific research programs developed by Lakatos (1970). He identifies three levels in an individual's cognitive organization that correspond to Lakatos's levels of metaphysical hard-core, protective belt, and actual research plans. The core level of an individual's cognitive, theoretical organization comprises schemata that are formed during childhood and adolescence, and which are held tacitly by the individual as unquestionable assumptions about important aspects of self and reality. The intermediate level of an individual's cognitive, theoretical organization consists of "protective" verbalizable descriptions of one's self, other people, and the world. Here, Liotti (1986, p. 98) stresses the polarized, dichotomous character of these constructions and explicitly relates them to Kelly's (1955) conceptualization of personal constructs. The explicit descriptions of the intermediate level function to protect the core assumptions an individual holds about self and reality. Finally, the peripheral level of individual cognitive, theoretical organization encompasses the plans of action and the problem-solving strategies the individual uses to navigate the demands of daily life. Appraisals, evaluations, interpretations, and reactions to daily events, while arising from a multilevel interaction between these events and all three levels of an individual's cognitive, theoretical organization are manifested at this peripheral level. Similar to the ways in which more peripheral propositions can be altered to preserve the core assumptions of a scientific theory (i.e., in light of contrary evidence), beliefs about self and one's circumstances can be altered while preserving the indispensable core unities of a self-theory.

In a similar vein, Guidano (1987, 1991) elaborates the complexity of self as co-evolving with a capacity for intersubjectivity in human relationships. The self envisioned by Guidano (1991) is a dynamic process of "construction and reconstruction of a reality capable of making consistent the ongoing experience of the ordering individual" (p. 5). Central to Guidano's dynamic organization is a dialectical interplay between the experiencing "I" and an explaining self, an interplay that results in a continuous reordering of self and reality. This kind of developmental analysis plays out in therapeutic methods in which clients attempt imaginal replications of affectively charged scenes from their past, scenes implicated in the construction of clients' current sense of self.

The metaphor of therapy as self-development also has been elaborated by Martin (1994) and Buirs and Martin (1997), who have incorporated Markus's theory of possible selves (1983;

Markus & Nurius, 1986; Markus & Wurf, 1987; Oyserman & Markus, 1990) into their formulations. As discussed in a previous chapter, Markus and her colleagues believe that an individual's complete self-theory (self-concept) actually is made up of various representations of self that are potentially available to the conscious awareness of the individual.

The third constructivist metaphor in psychotherapy, that of *therapy as conceptual revision* to mental schemas or frameworks, has been advanced consistently by cognitively oriented psychotherapy theorists and practitioners. For example, Albert Ellis (1962) attempted to integrate the Stoic philosophy of Epictetus into a practical guide for recognizing and eliminating basic irrational ideas that he thought were responsible for a wide range of human misery. Since then, Ellis and numerous other rational constructivists have developed this basic idea into a complex system of rational emotive and behavioral psychotherapy that attempts to reconstruct the basic beliefs of individuals along more rational-adaptive and functional lines (e.g., Dryden, 1984). Of course, a whole generation of applied psychologists since the early 1970s has practiced various forms of cognitive behavior modification in which the supposedly dysfunctional thoughts and behaviors of clients seeking psychotherapy are targeted for focused forms of therapeutic reconstruction and revision. Influential contributors to cognitive behavioral psychotherapy have included Meichenbaum (1977), Mahoney (1980, 1990) and Beck (1967, 1976).

Perhaps the largest body of contemporary empirical literature in psychotherapy from a cognitive behavioral perspective has been stimulated by Aaron Beck's (1967, 1976) approach to understanding and treating depression. Beck believes that depressive schemas are negative views (informal theories) of the self, the world, and the future. These negative schemas operate in the experience of depressed individuals to bias negatively their cognitive/perceptual processing and behavioral selection in ways that continuously confirm the content of these schemas. Empirical research in this tradition (e.g., Derry & Kuiper, 1981) has focused on analyzing the functions of depressive self-schemas, defined as hierarchically organized bodies of knowledge stored in clients' memories. A good deal of research (cf. Kuiper & Higgins, 1985) now exists that usually is interpreted as demonstrating how the negatively slanted, personal schemas (theories) of depressed clients bias their understandings and interpretations of their life experiences as essentially sad, meaningless, and hopeless, and lead to behavioral patterns of withdrawal, excessive criticism, and general miserableness. A wide variety of cognitive behavioral psychotherapeutic interventions has been developed and researched as possible means of altering such dysfunctional schemas (cf. Mahoney, 1995).

A fourth constructivistic metaphor for psychotherapy and psychotherapeutic change is that of *therapy as narrative reconstruction*. Narrative or storied approaches to understanding human change processes in general, have become extremely popular with psychotherapy researchers and scholars in the 1980s and 1990s. Narrative psychologists like Bruner (1986), Mair (1988), McAdams (1988), Polkinghorne (1988), Sarbin (1986), Howard (1989), Vogel (1994), and White and Epston (1990) have influenced recent depictions of psychotherapy as "life-story elaboration, adjustment, or repair" (Howard, 1991, p. 194). These recent developments have highlighted the contemporary relevance of earlier, slightly more socially constructionist construals of psychotherapy as an interpersonal, social process aimed at elaborating and revising the styles, scripts, and stories through which clients lead their lives (Adler, 1963; Berne, 1961; Rosen, 1982).

The final constructivist metaphor of *therapy as conversational elaboration* fits nicely with various construals of psychotherapy as narrative reconstruction and as schema revision. In psychotherapy, the therapeutic conversation has the potential of assisting clients to elaborate meanings resident in their personal schemas, theories, or stories. Proponents of the conversational elaboration metaphor regard humans as quintessentially language generating, defining their organization through discourse and negotiation. Meaning is seen to arise through communicative action, as much or more than residing within individual selves. In this regard, psychotherapy becomes a collaborative and creative implementation of language within a problem-solving, problem-organizing system. Systemic therapies practiced by a new generation of family therapists (Feixas, 1990; Penn, 1985; Procter, 1987) illustrate the conversational elaboration metaphor. Such approaches to psychotherapy highlight the role of the psychotherapist in elucidating and subtly challenging the contractual agreements, meanings, and organizations that solidify relationships within a family, sometimes in highly dysfunctional ways. The therapist functions as a conversational manager attempting to co-construct a new story with the family, one that has a sense of coherence and is perceived as relevant to the concerns of its members.

Clearly, cognitive constructivist work has been influential in psychotherapy theory, research, and practice. In several of the metaphors we have examined, especially the final metaphor of therapy as conversational elaboration, there exist possibilities for social constructionist incursions, but these remain for the most part underdeveloped. Nonetheless, the radical individualism and radical constructivism, replete in most psychotherapy literature, frequently have led critics (e.g., Taylor, 1989b; Szasz, 1961) to challenge the entire edifice of Western psychotherapy, its practitioners, and its organizations and institutions for placing undue emphasis on what such critics see as rather limited possibilities for significant human change resident in individuals who more realistically are better portrayed as overwhelmed by sociocultural practices inimical to their positive psychological functioning.

Few attempts exist to integrate social constructionist and cognitive constructivist thought in an understanding of psychotherapeutic practice. One exception is the work of William Lyddon (1995). Lyddon attempts to analyze the divergent philosophical bases of the various constructivist metaphors and theories existing in the area of psychotherapy. In particular, he employs assumptions associated with Pepper's (1942) taxonomy of world hypotheses to differentiate various forms of psychological constructivism he finds in psychotherapeutic theorizing. He concludes that while differences among these forms of constructivist psychology may be somewhat unsettling, they all might reflect viable accounts of different aspects of human knowing. A full understanding of the constructive nature of human knowing may require input from all such metaphors.

AN INTEGRATIVE PROPOSAL

Consistent with Lyddon's general approach, but also incorporating more decidedly social constructionist views, Martin (1994) attempted to conceptualize psychotherapeutic change in a manner generally consistent with the kind of bridging of social constructionism and cognitive constructivism advanced in this volume. We adopt much of Martin's earlier account in our own description of psychotherapeutic change.

The primary general implication that flows from our theoretical bridging of social constructionism and cognitive constructivism is that human development, learning, and change exhibit a kind of constrained or limited possibility. Our underdetermination thesis allows for the innovative emergence of new ways of thinking and acting, but the general sociocultural origins of these phenomena constrain these emergent possibilities. Our ability to learn from our encounters with previously unexperienced practices and forms of knowing always is imperfectly determined by our experiential pasts and what we have taken from them. Gadamer's (1960/1975) metaphor of fused horizons is apt here. Human learning and change may be viewed as the emergence of new horizons of understanding and/or being. These horizons are somewhat different from both the practices and forms resident in novel sociocultural experiences and those practices and forms resident in an individual's previous modes of understanding and being that have been drawn from past experience.

The constantly emergent individual is thus caught up in an ongoing dynamic process of fusion, immersed in the unfolding panorama of practical and epistemic sources potentially available in lived experience, in interaction with those already taken from such experience. With this general view in place, and in light of our summary of social constructionist and cognitive constructivist thought in the area of psychotherapy, we now offer the following description of psychotherapy and psychotherapeutic change. In our view, this description instantiates the metaphysical and epistemological arguments we have developed previously in a way that constitutes a progressive advance in understanding psychotherapy and psychotherapeutic change. Not only do we incorporate more of a social constructionist perspective than is common in extant theorizing in this area, but we integrate our account of psychotherapeutic change with a more streamlined, coherent rendering of what we retain of the kinds of constructivistic metaphors and accounts we briefly have surveyed.

In our view, psychotherapy is a somewhat unique, socially sanctioned interpersonal activity devoted to assisting individual members of a society to change (cf. Martin, 1994). We begin by assuming that human experience occurs in the context of cultural, social, interpersonal, and personal conversations and other relational practices. Human thought and forms of understanding are appropriated from these conversations and practices and internalized in individuals' memories and emergent understandings. Indeed, memories of past experience in conversations and relational practices act as primary mediational vehicles for the internalization of forms of thought and understanding. Personal theories emerge as systems of belief based on internalized forms of thought and understanding. Such theories about self, others, the world, and one's situation support and enable experiential, affective, motivational, and cognitive processes (including values, reasons, dispositions, and goals) on which human actions are based. When individuals' current theories and the actions they support do not permit the attainment of personal goals, acceptable resolutions to personal problems or concerns, or acceptable levels of personal coping, individuals suffer emotional upset and seek change.

As we already have indicated, psychotherapy is a unique form of social conversation and interpersonal activity that attempts to help individuals to alter their personal theories so as to permit more effective goal attainment, problem resolution, or personal coping. Psychotherapists work collaboratively with clients to elaborate clients' current theories through facilitating memory-mediated recall, interpretation, and analysis of past and current experiences and understandings in the context of the therapeutic conversation. Psychotherapists also work collaboratively with clients to help clients revise their theories, once these have been elaborated. Such revision is achieved by clients' internalization of the therapeutic conversations and activities through which their personal theories have been elaborated, interpreted, and analyzed. Ultimately, clients who have benefited from psychotherapeutic conversations and practices are potentially capable of contributing to the personal, interpersonal, social, and cultural contexts in which they exist in ways that alter these conversations, practices, and their experiences in them.

Having provided this straightforward summary of psychotherapeutic change in terms consistent with our attempt to bridge social constructionist and cognitive constructivistic accounts of psychological development in general, we want to stress that the constructive dynamics of psychotherapeutic change do not differ in kind from those more general constructive dynamics that we believe enable all human psychological development and change. We also want to stress that the quality and quantity of therapeutic change in any given case inevitably will depend on the nature (variety, depth, breadth, and so forth) of the lived experience afforded to an individual client prior to, during, and subsequent to experience in the psychotherapeutic context.

EMPIRICAL DEMONSTRATION

How clients in psychotherapy internalize therapeutic conversations and how such internalizations can become functional psychological tools for clients are illustrated in the following case study (Martin, 1987). The client was a 35-year-old woman who suffered verbal and physical abuse from a man with whom she lived. Immediately following each of eight sessions of therapy, the woman was asked to free associate to her own name and to her partner's name, brief phrases describing her problems and possible solutions to her problems. All of the client's associative responses were recorded on gummed labels—one response to each label. These labels then were returned to the client so that she could organize them on a sheet of laminated paper to indicate relationships among the words or phrases contained on the labels by placing related labels close to one another or by using marking pencils to draw connecting lines between labels or by both methods.

In this case study, the client's responses to the free association and conceptual mapping tasks clearly revealed her internalization of therapeutic conversations during the eight therapy sessions. Following the first session of therapy, her conceptual map of her problems consisted of a centrally located, self-referencing label ("me") connected directly to surrounding labels indicative of negative affect ("hopeless," "trapped," "afraid," "ashamed," "can't do anything right") and connected indirectly to clusters of labels representing her partner, her children, and her parents as well as her relationships with them. The labels offered no indication of understanding of or insight into her problems, or of possible strategies that might be engaged to address her problems. Following eight sessions of psychotherapy, the client produced a conceptual map of her problems that contained clear indications of both enhanced understanding and possible strategies of responding. In this last map, a centrally located, self-referencing label was connected directly to a cluster of labels representing her unwilling participation in a cycle of family violence in which her partner was represented as a dangerous batterer in need of help. Another cluster of labels emanating directly from the central self-referencing label identified strategic options available through a local women's center and through the supportive intervention of her extended family. Affective labels in this map referred to anger and worry, but also to hope.

Results obtained on the conceptual-mapping task employed in this case study, when set against transcriptions and tape recordings of the therapy sessions themselves, indicated a clear relationship between salient conversational themes during the course of therapy and the client's free-associative, conceptual-mapping responses following the therapy sessions. The therapeutic intervention focused primarily on clarifying and elaborating the client's affective reactions, providing information about relationship violence and men who batter women, and exploring options that would remove the client from her currently dysfunctional life circumstances. In this case, the conceptual-mapping responses of the client were interpreted as evidence of her internalization of these therapeutic conversations into her personal theory regarding her problems and possible solutions to them. The eventual ability of this client to extricate herself from the abusive relationship she had endured for so many years and to make more favorable arrangements for herself and her children was facilitated by this internalization process.

The dual legacy of experiential constraints and possibilities with respect to psychotherapeutic change is illustrated further in a recently conducted research study by a graduate student of the first author of this volume (Buirs & Martin, 1997). The question guiding this research concerned the extent to which the conversational construction of possible selves during psychotherapy is constrained by past and present extratherapeutic social, interpersonal experiences of clients. Six clients (all substance abusers) expressed, explored, and attempted to synthesize their feelings and experiences during two role plays in which they imagined two future scenarios. In one scenario, the negative possible self role-play, the clients imagined that their problems with substance abuse remained unchanged. In the other, the positive possible self role-play, they imagined that these problems had been overcome. All six clients were more likely to express directly feelings and experiences in the negative possible self role-play than in the positive possible self role-play.

Such a result is consistent with a strong social constructionist view that would locate the origins of current psychological experience in one's history of experience in relevant social contexts. The fact that all six clients were active substance abusers probably made it easier for them to enact the negative possible self role-plays with greater expressions of feeling and experience than they displayed during the less familiar, positive possible self role-plays. Nonetheless, there were dramatic and we believe reliable indications that clients' participation in the less familiar, positive possible self role-plays enabled them to synthesize newly realized or more fully recognized feelings and experiences more so than in the negative possible self role-plays. We believe that this second result provides some confirmation of the possibility that psychotherapeutic constructions might be internalized by clients as sources of potential revision to their existing theoretical and experiential beliefs and practices, supplementing and augmenting emergent capabilities of active functional memory and imagination. Our faith in this interpretation is strengthened further by the many examples of clients' recollection and apparent internalization of psychotherapeutic discourse and experience provided by Martin (1994).

Considered more generally, we understand psychotherapy as a human creation grounded in the historical and contemporary renderings that we give it by virtue of our cultural, social, and personal notions of psychological health and healing. Psychotherapy is part of our own sociocultural tradition of conversation and practice, one by which we attempt to alter our personal theories about ourselves and our lives. These are theories we have extracted from our lifelong participation in our families, our friendships and relationships, our societies, and our cultures, but which currently do not serve us well in assisting us to reach our goals, resolve our problems, or cope with current life situations. In this sense, psychotherapy is simply a professionalized version of our ongoing quest to extract more meaningful understandings of ourselves and our world from our interactions in the physical and sociocultural worlds we occupy and to which we contribute.

5

Applying a Psychology of Possibility and Constraint

Education

*U*nlike theories of practice in psychotherapy, theories of educational development and practice display a fairly even balance of social constructionist and cognitive constructivist thought. Perhaps because of educators' joint concerns with the transmission of human cultural accomplishment and wisdom, and with the nurturing and realization of individual capacities for critical thought and self-fulfillment, most educational theories emphasize appropriate immersion in accepted forms and content of knowledge and processes of knowing in ways intended to stimulate individual and collective capacities for remembering, understanding, and creating. Nonetheless, relative differences in emphasis on sociocultural versus individual processes and phenomena frequently erupt in heated disputation among educators, students, and others affected by educational policies and practices. Classic and continuing debates between advocates of student-centered versus teacher- or curriculum-centered teaching, direct versus indirect instruction, the teaching of knowledge and content versus the teaching of processes of thinking and knowing, all reflect such underlying tension.

A major task taken up by many philosophers of education in this and previous centuries has been to conceptualize education in a way that somehow steers a middle course between an unthinking, anti-intellectual emphasis on the learner, as found in some progressive educational rhetoric (e.g., "I teach children, not mathematics"), and an overly rigid, unresponsive attempt to shape learners to strict, pre-established norms. One such example is found in the work of R. S. Peters (1966). What Peters saw as lacking in both progressivist and technocist instrumentalist accounts of education was "the notion that [students' cognitive structures] develop out of, and as a response to, public traditions enshrined in the language, concepts, beliefs, and rules of a society" (p. 49). In Peters's view, the task of the educator is to initiate students into this public body of shared understandings and awareness, an initiation that presupposes nonsubjective standards to which both learner and teacher are accountable. Progressivists' focus on the individual child causes them to ignore the fact that the development of mind takes place and makes sense only within a social, intersubjective domain. On the other hand, an exclusive concern with molding the individual to conform to static pre-existing content and forms of knowing leads to an education that is impersonal, sterile, lacking in creativity, and possibly morally suspect. Peters's metaphor of initiation is intended to connote a way of working out a required reconciliation between child-centered and content-centered approaches to education. Peters's fundamental task was to formulate a conception of education that paid due respect to the learner without losing sight of the fact that education is concerned with the initiation of the learner into a public world of practices of knowing and understanding. For Peters, education implies a transmission of worthwhile knowledge that is not inert, but which results in a cognitive perspective that transforms the outlook of the individual.

In many ways, the work of Peters (1966) is quite consistent with the view of educational development and change that flows from our theory of human psychological development. Our descriptions and explanations of the ways in which forms and content of thought emerge from internalized conversational and other relational practices through the mediation of emergent and developing capacities for memory and imagination provides a psychological framework within which Peters's compromise of appropriate educational initiation might play out. Our position makes it clear that an initiation of young learners into the disciplinary understandings and awarenesses of intellectual culture and history need not lead to static regurgitation of past knowledge and ways of knowing, but can provide the required psychological tools for moving beyond the accomplishments of the past, through creative synthesis, analysis, and extension of past and current forms and content of knowledge that now constitute the essential raw material for intellectual change and innovation.

Joining our psychological explanation with Peters's philosophical positions results in an overall view of education that requires the sensible use of appropriate methods and procedures for transmitting relevant knowledge to young learners in ways that do not violate the willingness and voluntary participation of those learners, and in ways that gradually and increasingly, over time, model the kind of critical reflection likely to stimulate creative, innovative elaborations, extensions, and challenges to our knowledge and ways of knowing. Of course, such initiation into critical reflective capacities follows upon initiation into more established, conventional ways of thinking and knowing. To do otherwise would be a recipe for intellectual chaos and nihilism. Again, following Peters, the development of mind is sensible only within a pre-existing social, intersubjective consensus. However, as he or she gradually becomes a full participant in this consensus, the learner is not entirely constrained to accept passively all aspects of the consensus view. Indeed, if our thesis of underdetermination implies anything, it implies that learners exposed to, and participating in, the kind of educational developmental sequence and pattern we have described, inevitably are capable of moving beyond such consensus views in their own thinking, speculating, imagining, and eventually in their accomplishments as mature participants in full-blown, intellectual activity.

It is relatively easy to imagine a set of specific propositions, similar to those we previously offered as a description and explanation of psychotherapy and psychotherapeutic change, intended to illuminate specific processes of education and educational development within our general theory of human psychological development. Such propositions obviously would include attention to the ways in which memory and imagination develop out of appropriate immersion and participation in relevant domains of knowledge, and serve to mediate further acquisition and development of increasingly sophisticated forms and processes of knowledge and knowledge construction. However, we believe that, by this time, readers are quite familiar with our developmental template and various instantiations of it. Instead, we want to turn to contemporary debates within education between advocates of sociocultural and radically constructivistic views of teaching and learning to demonstrate how the kind of compromise described philosophically by Peters, and supported psychologically by our theory of human development, has escaped serious consideration in most such debates. In so doing, we hope to illustrate the relevance of our views on education, consistent with our theory of human psychological development, for moving beyond much contemporary debate concerning appropriate means and ways of fostering the intellectual and moral development of learners in educational contexts.

SOCIOCULTURAL VERSUS CONSTRUCTIVIST ACCOUNTS OF EDUCATIONAL DEVELOPMENT

The cognitive constructivist view of education is that students actively construct their ways of knowing as they strive to maintain coherence in their personal theories of the world (von

Glasersfeld, 1987, 1989, 1992). Empirical support for this constructivist viewpoint comes from studies that document significant qualitative differences in the understandings that different students develop in the same educational setting, understandings that frequently differ in important ways from those the teacher intended to convey (e.g., Confrey, 1990; Hiebert & Carpenter, 1992).

Opposed to the constructivist view is a sociocultural position that emphasizes the situated nature of intellectual activity and learning. Socioculturalist theorists eschew purely cognitive levels of analysis in an attempt to combat what they perceive as an unwarranted individualistic emphasis in constructivist theories of education (e.g., Brown, Collins, & Duguid, 1989; Greeno, 1991). Socioculturalists claim empirical support from studies demonstrating that individuals' learning and intellectual activity are affected dramatically by their participation in cultural practices as varied as completing assignments in school and shopping in malls.

Both sociocultural and constructivist theorists of education highlight the importance of activity in human learning and development. However, sociocultural theorists focus on students' participation in culturally sanctioned classroom and extracurricular practices, whereas constructivists attend mostly to individual students' perceptual and conceptual processes. Constructivists analyze thought in terms of processes located in the individual. Sociocultural theorists adopt the individual-in-social-action as their focal unit.

The theoretical basis for contemporary sociocultural theory in education comes from the work of Vygotsky and other Russian activity theorists (Nunes, 1992). As we saw in Chapter 2, Vygotsky (1934/1986, 1978) emphasized the importance of social interaction with more knowledgeable others in the zone of proximal development. Through such interactions, socioculturally developed sign systems are internalized as psychological tools for thinking. Contemporary followers of Vygotsky speak of cognitive apprenticeship (e.g., Brown, Collins, & Duguid, 1989), legitimate peripheral participation (Lave & Wenger, 1991), or negotiation of meaning in the construction zone (Newman, Griffin, & Cole, 1989). In all these construals, learning is located in participation in cultural practices. Sociocultural theorists of education focus on the kinds of social engagement that enable students to participate in the activities of the expert in a graduated manner over time.

Constructivists in education adopt the work of Jean Piaget (1954, 1970) as a basis for their theorizing about student learning and development. For example, von Glasersfeld (1992) incorporates the Piagetian notions of assimilation and accommodation, and uses the term knowledge to refer to those sensory-motor and conceptual operations that have proved viable in the knower's experience. Here, traditional correspondence theories of truth give way to accounts that relate truth or correctness to the utility or effectiveness of a learner's cognitive activity and organization. In this model, perturbations that the cognizing subject generates relative to a purpose or goal are viewed as powerful intellectual motivators, as the driving forces of cognitive development. The role of the teacher is to create or to facilitate productive forms of perturbation in learners. Learning itself is understood as a process by which the learner reorganizes his or her understanding and cognitive activity to eliminate perturbations.

While some radical constructivists (e.g., von Glasersfeld, 1992) focus almost exclusively on learners' construction of ways of knowing, with little direct reference to the status of what is known, other more moderate constructivists (e.g., Bauersfeld, 1988) emphasize that while learning is fundamentally a matter of subjective reconstruction, the raw materials for such reconstruction are societal means and models through which meaning is negotiated in social interactions. Thus, more moderate forms of constructivism in educational theory and research seem to entail recognition of the need to accept the essentially social constructionist thesis that relevant processes of individual learning occur in a context of implicit and explicit negotiations of knowledge and meaning in a social, public arena of interactions with others, and with various traditions of knowledge and knowing.

Nonetheless, both radical and moderate forms of constructivism differ in the kinds of problems and issues they address, from emphases found in sociocultural educational theory. For example, a sociocultural analysis of a classroom episode likely would locate the episode within a broader activity system of the school as a social institution. Immediate interactions between teacher and students would be understood within this broader consideration. Thus, socioculturalists such as Lave and Wenger (1991) claim that their "concept of legitimate peripheral participation provides a framework for bringing together theories of situated activity and theories about the production and reproduction of the social order" (p. 47). A basic tenet of such work is that it is inappropriate to fixate on qualitative differences in individual thinking apart from a consideration of broader sociocultural contexts. In other words, students' participation in, and interpretations of, school tasks are seen to reflect qualitative differences in the communities in which they participate and develop.

By contrast, constructivists focus directly on the quality of individual interpretive and conceptual activity, especially the development of ways of knowing. When learners' interactions with classroom norms and practices are considered, the burden of explanation in constructivist accounts of educational development still falls on models of individual students' self-organization, and analyses of the internal processes by which these cognitively active individuals construe a classroom situation. From one perspective, the focus is on sociocultural bases of personal experience. From the other, the focus is on the interpretation and construal of sociocultural processes by cognitively active individuals.

A major difficulty facing educational constructivists is how to account for learners' internalizations from the social realm to the cognitive realm. The difficulty springs from the fact that the interpersonal relations that are to be internalized are located outside the learner. From this point of view, the problem of explaining how relations that are real for the detached observer get into the experiential world of the child appears intractable. The underlying assumption is that material to be learned somehow is brought across a barrier into the mind of the child. However, how this is done is not specified and constitutes a deep problem for constructivist theorists of education.

On the other hand, a significant problem encountered by sociocultural theorists of education is how to account for human learning that displays creative advance that goes beyond anything available currently in the sociocultural practices and ways of knowing in which a learner has participated. While significantly creative accomplishments probably are rare, their existence and importance are undeniable, and the failure of sociocultural accounts to offer any convincing explanation of them constitutes a significant difficulty.

Constructivists argue that sociocultural theorists do not adequately account for the process of learning that entails the possibility of creative advance. Sociocultural theorists retort that constructivists fail to explain the production and reproduction of the practices of schooling and the social order. "The challenge of relating actively constructing students, the local microculture [of classrooms and schools], and the established practices of the broader community requires that adherents to each perspective acknowledge the potential positive contributions of the other perspective" (Cobb, 1994, p. 18).

BRIDGING SOCIOCULTURAL AND CONSTRUCTIVIST ACCOUNTS OF EDUCATIONAL DEVELOPMENT

It is precisely in its ability to respond to this kind of challenge that we believe our theory of human psychological development makes a potentially powerful contribution to educational theory and practice. For many educationists, Cobb's (1994, 1995) attempts to reconcile sociocultural and cognitive theories of educational development came as a breath of fresh air. Although, as Phillips (1995) has reasonably pointed out, much constructivist talk in education seems to fail to recognize fundamental differences in the sociocultural and cognitive perspectives with which

Cobb was concerned, a careful reconciliation of these perspectives, if possible, would be understandably attractive to educational practitioners and theorists. After all, few these days doubt either that students actively construct their ways of knowing as they strive to maintain coherence in their personal theories of the world (von Glasersfeld, 1989, 1996), or that learning and intellectual activity are situated and unfold within social and cultural contexts and practices (Lave & Wenger, 1991). Why not simply accept both points of view to the extent that they are seen to provide useful guidance relative to the various purposes of educators, and be done with it? Unfortunately, such uncritical, unfettered pragmatism fails to recognize that the claims of socioculturalists and cognitivists are not so readily joined.

There is little in the way of metaphysical argument in Cobb's (1994) initial piece. However, in his subsequent rejoinder to Smith (1995), Cobb (1995) makes it quite clear that his pragmatic perspectivism leans toward the socioculturalists' penchant for sociocultural-psychological monism. Here, he declares that the focus of his own theorizing "is on the world of collective activity within which members of a community live their lives. The idea that students are already in the social world in fact implies that they are already acting in a taken-as-shared world of signification" (p. 26). Cobb (1995) then goes on to label his approach as nondualistic in that "human activity and the world are mutually constitutive" (p. 26). Apparently, Cobb has in mind a kind of metaphysics that holds that sociocultural activity and the activity of mind are simply two aspects of the same kind of stuff. However, beyond offering this rather cryptic hint, Cobb again prefers to keep his discourse away from the metaphysical.

Cobb's (1994, 1995) pragmatic perspectivism asks educators to refuse a forced choice between socioculturalist and cognitivist views of educational theory and practice. Cobb's injunction is supported forcefully by Bruner's (1996) recent caution: "To sneer at the power of culture to shape man's mind and to abandon our efforts to bring this power under human control is to commit moral suicide" (pp. 184–185). By clarifying possible ways in which socioculturally developed and spawned capabilities for memory and imagination can mediate learners' acquisition of forms and ways of knowing, our theory resolves the difficulty experienced by existing cognitivist theories of education in explaining how knowledge and processes of learning become incorporated into students' developing minds. At the same time, our under-determination thesis, aided by our conception of relative spatiotemporal differences between sociocultural practices and the activities of mind, enables an understanding of creative aspects of learning that goes beyond anything available in past and current sociocultural educational practices.

What we hope to add to pleas, such as Cobb's (1994, 1995) and Bruner's (1996) for theoretical and practical balance between cultural and cognitive perspectives in education, is a metaphysical foundation that not only celebrates both perspectives, but which explains how culture and cognition are necessarily related and mutually constitutive. With such a metaphysics in place, there simply is no forced choice between socioculturalist and cognitivist frameworks, nor is there any possibility of a detached educationist viewpoint from which to select one or the other frame according to immediate purposes (as suggested by Cobb, 1994, 1995). Rather, culture and mind require and constantly transform each other in ways that educators might come to understand better if they give up metaphysically misguided attempts to reduce either one to the other.

We previously have acknowledged the kinship we perceive between our view of educational development as an instantiation of our more general theory of human psychological development, and the philosophical writings of R. S. Peters (1966). We also want to point to what we see as a close connection between our view and that advanced initially by John Dewey (1929, 1931/1964), and developed more recently by individuals like Prawat (1993; Prawat & Floeden, 1994). Prawat (1993) interprets Dewey's views on education as a kind of "idea-based social constructivism" (p. 5). Idea-based social constructivism assigns a high priority in education to important ideas developed within established intellectual and academic traditions. The teacher's task, according to this view, is to create communities of discourse in which students participate to figure out and apply these big ideas. Ideally, the classroom is a center of lively discussion and interaction where learners and teacher engage in animated conversations about important intellectual matters. In such a setting, "teacher and student form a learning community, keeping one eye on the discipline, and the other on the real world phenomena [ideas] they seek to understand" (Prawat, 1995, p. 20). The instantiation of our theory of human psychological development within this general neo-Deweyan viewpoint helps to understand how the two-way street described by Prawat is possible. In fact, there are two major aspects to this process. The first is sociocultural and occurs as teachers and learners discuss ideas in the social context of the classroom. The second involves students' appropriation of these discussions and ideas through the mediation of their own memory and imagination, eventually using these ideas as tools with which to describe, understand, and explain phenomena that otherwise might remain hidden or mysterious to them and possibly to others as well.

Nuthall and Alton-Lee (1995) provide an illustration of how classroom learning takes place through processes of conversational elaboration, appropriation, memorial and imaginative mediation, and active interpretation and construction. As part of an extensive study of New Zealand students (nine to twelve years of age), Nuthall and Alton-Lee conducted interviews to investigate the basis for students' answers given on multiple choice achievement tests. According to Nuthall and Alton-Lee, a consistent relationship emerged between students' recollections of relevant classroom episodes and choice of test items.

Interviews conducted immediately after administration of tests demonstrated that students used their episodic memories of specific classroom experiences in which they learned content (in addition to the content itself) in answering 60 to 75 percent of test items. Drawing on their recollections of classroom episodes to generate answers, students recalled classroom conversations and physical details of classrooms in addition to directly relevant experiences in curricular activities. Nuthall and Alton-Lee (1995) report that students' descriptions of their classroom experiences sometimes were given in considerable detail while, on other occasions, students provided abstracted or summarized accounts. Additionally, for 9 to 15 percent of test items, students used their episodic memories of out-of-class experiences, such as conversations with others, television, and books, to generate answers, while 10 to 15 percent of test items were selected ostensibly on the basis of inference and logical deduction. Subsequent tests and interviews conducted a year later revealed that students persist in using episodic memories to generate answers to test items (55 percent), and their attempts to use deduction from conceptually related knowledge or experience increased to 25 percent.

Particularly instructive are the many transcribed excerpts provided by Nuthall and Alton-Lee (1993, 1995) detailing students' appropriations of specific classroom conversations and the ways in which students rely on their episodic memories and imaginative abilities to render interpretations. For example, when asked about the basis for knowing the name of the space between two high pressure areas on a weather map, a student replied:

> Yeah, Mr. B said, I think it's a trough because he said, he used, he put trough and ridge or trough and ditch on the [black]board for us. Something was low, and something was high. He used one of those. He used trough on it. (Nuthall & Alton-Lee, 1995, p. 218)

Subsequently in the interview, the student rejected the correct term, "trough," despite remembering the classroom episode. The student stated: "Yeah, I don't think it is that though . . . I thought it was something a horse drunk out of" (Nuthall & Alton-Lee, 1995, p. 218). As in the case above, the excerpts further show how students also bring to bear linguistic knowledge, socially sustained standards of reason, and critical judgment to assess the correctness of ideas and information given in their episodic memories especially when contradiction is apparent between information derived from recollected events and deductive reasoning. The work of Nuthall and Alton-Lee depicts the highly individual, experiential, and personalized nature of students' learning and, at the same time, how such learning is socioculturally charged.

The grand view of education that follows from our bridging of social constructionism and cognitive constructivism is one in which an individual's sociocultural experiences are expanded and placed within a larger horizon. Through education, familiarity and interest are cultivated in issues, problems, perspectives, and in ways of life that might be quite distant from one's own. In all of this, there is and must be a genuine attempt to understand one's place within a larger world community, and to come to understand and care for the very best it has produced in the way of moral, cultural, social, and epistemic accomplishments throughout its history. Such a conception is intended to maximize possibilities for human learning and creativity, while reducing unnecessarily narrow sociocultural, experiential constraints on human innovation and change.

As in Gadamer's (1960/1975) rendering of the concept of *Bildung*, the idea of self-formation contained in such a view of education is decentered from an isolated, psychological ego. To the extent to which individuals educated in this sense can integrate their understanding of others within their own self-understanding, they develop a wider, more differentiated view, one typified by sensitivity, subtlety, and a capacity for discrimination. In this process of becoming more broadly cultured, we acquire the ability to engender more and varied opportunities for continued and sustained development, as well as a set of largely tacit but critical capacities for such things as tact, taste, and judgment. These are not merely cognitive ways of knowing and behaving, but are embodied forms of knowing, built up over time into a set of habits that reflects a person's transcendence of individual ego, and a self-formation genuinely tied to the shared values, goals, accomplishments, and visions of wider communities.

Lave and Wenger (1991) recently have described education and learning in terms of a learner's initially peripheral, and gradually more and more central entry into, and eventual full participation in, communities of practice. This kind of graduated participation, membership, and eventual possibility for forging innovation in relevant communities, is quite consistent with the general educational implications with which we are concerned. However, if one views education as a gradual and graduated participation into the practices and forms of multifaceted intellectual life per se, greater emphasis probably should be given to the development of a kind of progressively emergent capacity for critical reflection. Learners (from kindergarten to university) should be expected initially to enter into, and participate with, established practices and forms, and gradually should be helped to challenge, elaborate, and revise such positions in light of an ever-expanding array of other possibilities and considerations, all within a genuine spirit of caring for the activities, practices, criticisms, and transformations that define intellectual life.

A basic challenge for educators then is to provide appropriately graduated opportunities for learners' participation in relevant communities that not only occasion immersion in the practices of these communities, but also promote transformation and progressive change in communal practices through learners' eventual critical and innovative participation as mature individuals with full community membership. The fundamental challenge of individual educational development is revealed as a developmental challenge facing our educational and broader communities. Clearly, we cannot educate successfully in schools where critical, intellectual life is extinct, or where there is blatant disregard for individuals and their rights and responsibilities. The general and more specific relations in our sociocultural practices that make possible individual cognitive development and learning, demand that we see ourselves in the communities we inhabit, and that our efforts are directed consistently toward improving upon and perhaps transcending that vision.

In light of the metaphysical bridging of socioculturalism and cognitivism we have attempted, education can be construed as the creation of a context in which students' sociocultural experiences are elaborated and placed within a larger horizon. Educators strive to foster awareness, understanding, and interest in issues, perspectives, and in ways of life often quite alien from those of learners. It is apparent that for this endeavor to succeed there must be a genuine intention to understand one's place within the broader context of the world and its constitutive communities, and to come to understand and care for the moral, cultural, social, and epistemic accomplishments human history has bequeathed us. Education, thusly conceived, entails maximizing resources and possibilities for human learning and creativity while, at the same time, limiting unnecessarily restrictive sociocultural constraints on human innovation and change. In this sense, education is fundamentally concerned with the fostering of human creativity and innovation, a topic to which we now turn directly.

CREATIVITY AND INNOVATION

Our theses of underdetermination and shifting ontology cast light on the dynamically mutable and emergent nature of human psychology. In contrast to a conception of psychological functions and processes as precast and static, our account illuminates the imminent quality ostensible in psychological development, thought, action, and experience.

As a topic of inquiry, creativity not only has generated voluminous empirical research, but psychologists and educators also have spilt a great deal of ink attempting to set down what precisely is entailed by the concept. The creativity literature is rife with debate over what constitutes an adequate definition. While this lack of conceptual agreement might be seen as counterproductive, and perhaps a lamentable state of affairs, Torrance (1988) finds solace in the suggestion that it is part of the enigmatic makeup of creativity to resist attempts to exact a definition. A long-time investigator of creativity, Torrance concludes:

Creativity defies precise definition. This conclusion does not bother me at all. In fact, I am quite happy with it. Creativity is almost infinite. It involves every sense—sight, smell, hearing, feeling, taste, and even perhaps the extrasensory. Much of it is unseen, nonverbal, and unconscious. Therefore, even if we had a precise conception of creativity, I am certain we would have difficulty putting it into words. (p. 43)

There is something undeniably distinctive and experientially tangible in the phenomenology of creating, and in audiences' appreciation of the creative accomplishments of others. However, agreeing upon and articulating precisely what that something is, or what brings it about, has proven troublesome. Creativity seems to be found in every corner of human enterprise, and to encompass the full range of our sensory capabilities. In addition to obstacles to definition arising from this pervasiveness and breadth, there are the intractable difficulties one inevitably encounters when attempting to specify fully the necessary and sufficient criteria of any concept (Wittgenstein, 1953). Further, as we discuss subsequently, aspects of creative accomplishment also are subject to a shifting ontology and a kind of underdetermination, conditions of possibility arising within the developmental context that we claim provide some purchase on the emergent characteristics of human psychological and sociocultural phenomena, but which make absolute a priori description and prediction of these phenomena an unrealistic aim for social science (see ch. 3).

However, while creativity may defy strict formal definition, this in no way diminishes our desire to make sense of it and to articulate our conception of it. Comprehending our uniquely human ability to create and innovate with the aid of an intentional reflexive consciousness not only sheds light on the course of our collective history, but also, on our capacity to deal with the present and future. We propose that the shifting ontology and underdetermination of psychological phenomena allow for the emergence of creativity, just as they allow for learning and psychological change. However, while all creative acts are transformations, not all transformations can be regarded as creative acts. In order for an individual transformation to be worthy of the label "creative," it must manifest a particular kind of significance that is not necessarily found in learning or psychological change.

Creative acts are the acts of individual agents, and a person may comprehend his or her action to be creative. However, what distinguishes creative acts from other acts is a certain kind of value that is assessed according to particular standards of quality and originality. An individual may recognize this value in his or her own endeavor. However, it also is conceivable that he or she may simply overrate or exaggerate the merit of the idea or act. Thus, there is the sociocultural demand that creative acts and ideas be authenticated. In order for this to occur, individual transformations must be published, that is, brought under the light of public scrutiny and subjected to the judgments of others according to the critical canons of the day.

Thus, while human creativity requires individual agentic transformations, sociocultural practices constrain the emergent possibility of individuals' creativity in two ways. First, sociocultural practices provide forms that enable the development of an intentional reflexive consciousness. These forms serve as the psychological basis for the kinds of decisions individuals make in bringing about the private and public expression of creative transformations. Second, certain sociocultural practices constitute a milieu of critique in which personal transformations are assessed with regard to their value and creative merit.

In what follows, we elaborate the way in which a developmental perspective, and our theses of underdetermination and shifting ontology, can contribute to interpreting human creativity and innovation. However, we first sketch a background of issues involved in a central debate about the nature of creativity, one which we believe our ideas help to advance.

Individual and Sociocultural Orientations in Creativity Research

The notion that creativity is a characteristic of exceptional individuals, and that it is brought about by a special attribute of their mental processes, has a long history in psychological research. Psychologists' attempts to study the creative characteristics and processes of individuals first took root in the psychometric

tradition. Psychometric pioneers in creativity research, such as Torrance (1962, 1966, 1972) and Guilford (1950, 1967; Guilford, Wilson, & Christensen, 1952), argued that intelligence and creativity are each *sui generis* mental capacities, and they attempted to devise psychometric methods that would distinguish individuals comparatively according to a presumed, predetermined potential or trait for creative thought. For example, Guilford proposed that while some individuals are predisposed to providing conventional solutions to problems, others are prone to generating solutions that are more idiosyncratic, fashioned from unusual and unique associations. In the wake of a growing faith in the validity of psychometry to distinguish between intelligence and creativity, and a proliferation of creativity measures, individuals were categorized under rubrics such as "convergers" or "divergers" (corresponding to a distinction of Guilford's).

Some early creativity researchers also sought to identify definitive personality traits of individuals thought to be creative, as well as features of the creative process, by examining the accounts creative individuals gave of themselves, or descriptions of them given by their personal associates (e.g., Barron, 1969; Ghiselin, 1952/1985; MacKinnon, 1962). Another initial stream of investigation employed psychoanalytic interpretation to uncover the specific sublimatory or neurotic impulses presumed to motivate individuals to commit creative acts (e.g., Freud, 1908/ 1948; Hartmann, 1939; Kris, 1952; Kubie, 1958).

The methodological individualism undergirding these early forays into the study of creativity still prevails in much of mainstream contemporary creativity research. Many of the investigative themes of earlier research programs simply have been recast in a more contemporary, cognitivist mold. Most contemporary cognitivists posit a creative individual's superior constructive ability to identify, define or redefine, and solve problems by fashioning internal representations of "problem spaces." These internal structures then are navigated cognitively in a search for solutions through the use of analogies and other conceptual tools that enable the forming of unique and productive associations (e.g., Boden, 1990, 1994; Johnson-Laird, 1988; Mumford, Mobley,

Uhlman, Reiter-Palmon, & Doares, 1991; Mobley, Doares, & Mumford, 1992; Rostan, 1994; Simon, 1988; Sternberg, 1988).

Generally speaking, cognitivist programs of research conceptualize creativity as a special case of everyday problem-solving grounded in a basic mode of rule-governed thinking common among ordinary individuals. This assumption is particularly evident in attempts to duplicate creative problem-solving processes employing computational models (e.g., Boden, 1990, 1994; Johnson-Laird, 1988; Langley, Simon, Bradshaw, & Zytkow, 1987). Such attempts to model mental processes computationally rest on the Cartesian assumption of radical dualism that places heavy emphasis in psychological explanation on the individual functioning in isolation.

Reminiscent of Guilford's (1950, 1967) conjecture that divergence is a defining attribute of the thinking processes of creative individuals, the cognitivist perspective holds that the creative problem-solving process differs from ordinary problem-solving by virtue of the creative individual's ability to generate an increased number of novel combinations of concepts in search of solutions. This proposed increased cognitive flexibility and generativity, with less reliance on habitual associations in creative individuals' thinking processes, has been discussed in terms of a number of strongly related and often indistinguishable mental factors, including field dependence/independence (Noppe & Gallagher, 1977), synthetic and analytic thought (Feist, 1991), cognitive complexity (Quinn, 1980), cognitive style (Noppe, 1985), and ideational fluency and effort (Basadur & Thompson, 1986).

Other lines of study that emphasize the creative individual's special cognitive attributes have been concerned with locus of motivation (i.e., intrinsic versus extrinsic) (Amabile, 1983), characteristics such as stubbornness and the ability to persevere in the face of opposition to one's ideas (Perkins, 1981), or the notably intense periods of immersion and engagement (i.e., "flow states") reported by creative individuals that mark their creative process experientially (Csikszentmihalyi, 1990). Some contemporary cognitively oriented researchers also have conducted biographical studies of renowned creative individuals, with the aim of tracing pivotal influences in the developmental course of the creator's construction of ideational meanings and schemata that led to his or her innovation (e.g., Gardner, 1993; Gruber & Davis, 1988).

Against the traditional individualistic emphasis in creativity research, a new generation of research (e.g., Csikszentmihalyi, 1988; Gigerenzer, 1994; Lubeck & Bidell, 1988; Schaffer, 1994; Simonton, 1988; Smolucha and Smolucha, 1992; Weisberg, 1993) has drawn attention to the political, historical, developmental, and sociocultural dimensions of creativity, specifically the indispensable role that socioculturally defined domains of practice, critical canons, and other individuals play in the creator's accomplishment. Socioculturally oriented researchers argue that the criteria for making judgments about the creative value of something are intrinsically public and collective. In other words, an act takes on significance as creative only within the context of a socially organized domain of practice with its own conventions and norms of justification and critique.

Sociocultural researchers contend that innovation is dependent on the creator's immersion in, and acquisition of, the conventional knowledge and particular symbolic systems of a socioculturally defined domain of practice. From this perspective, innovations do not arise *ex nihilo* (cf. Perkins, 1988), nor can they be construed as the product of the exclusive efforts of a solo individual. Rather, innovations build on socioculturally accumulated wisdom and the knowledge of others to whom the creator is indebted. As Smolucha and Smolucha (1992) state with regard to the myth of the heroic creator whose innovations owe only to his or her individual efforts:

American cultural ideology is heavily influenced by Renaissance notions of the individuality of man, and by Rousseau's belief in the nobility of man in his natural condition. This has led many psychologists to underestimate the extent to which the founders of major theoretical paradigms introjected concepts from other theories into their own, and the extent to which their work was therefore a collaborative effort. The resultant "cult of originality" has perpetuated the idea that major theoretical paradigms are the products of a single individual's creativity rather than cumulative, cultural products. It should be acknowledged that a new theoretical synthesis often owes as much to its historical predecessors as it does to the individual who performs the synthesis. (p. 91)

It seems inconceivable that scientific or artistic innovations might be achieved without significant knowledge of the extant symbolic systems, forms of expression, and modes of practice comprising the particular discipline or field of endeavor in which the innovation occurs. Indeed, Gardner (1993) claims that for a breakthrough to occur in any established discipline, at least a decade of intensive immersion and study is required. Socioculturalists claim that taking a developmental and historical perspective in viewing individuals' creative accomplishments reveals the inextricable influence and involvement of the contributions of others.

Relatedly, it also is argued that a purely individualistic conception of creativity occludes the point that talent simply is insufficient to account for an individual's creative success. As well as the contribution of ideas, there are additional ways in which others contribute to the emergence of an innovation. Zuckerman (1977) contends that in the case of scientific discoveries, for example, the level of accomplishment and distinction of an innovator's mentors, and the level of financial and collegial support provided the innovator during his or her apprenticeship, can lead to a certain "accumulation of advantage" (p. 250) that contributes to his or her rise over equally talented, but less advantaged peers.

Further, socioculturalists argue that whether or not something can be deemed creative depends on its evaluation and acceptance by others. For something to count as an innovation, its value must be assessed favorably in light of canons prevailing in the zeitgeist of the era. In support of this point, it is not uncommon for scientific and artistic achievements not to be recognized as ground breaking until many years after their formulation. An oft cited example is the original publication of Mendel's work in

1866, which was not considered to constitute a major discovery until nearly three decades later. Mendel's ideas came to prominence in 1900 as a result of the retrospective recognition of their applicability to rising debates among European scientists concerning biometrics and saltationism (Brannigan, 1981). Likewise, Rembrandt was not revered by his contemporaries. It was not until many years later, after art historians had interpreted his work within the progressive historical context of European painting, that his work attained its illustrious stature (Alpers, 1988).

Brannigan, among other sociologists of science and art, promotes a shift away from a focus on the mind of the individual creator in explanations of creativity and innovation. He argues that greater attention ought to be paid to the important sociocultural criteria and traditions used by others in interpreting and authorizing something as an innovation. "Events are discoveries not in virtue of how they appear in the mind, but how they are defined in and by a cultural criterion" (Brannigan, 1981, p. 90).

In light of the socioculturalist critique, the individualistic ideology on which traditional creativity research programs and contemporary cognitivist theories of creativity rest puts an overly heroic twist on individuals' creativity. The result is the obfuscation of important political, historical, social, cultural, and developmental considerations that mark the role of interpersonal relations in creative accomplishment, and which both make possible and constrain an individual's innovation.

Not unlike our previous discussions of research and theory in psychotherapy and education, the contemporary study of creativity is marked by a split between perspectives that can be assimilated roughly under cognitive constructivist and social constructionist rubrics. Cognitive constructivists tend to emphasize the agentic individual acting in isolation, and his or her capacity to construct creative solutions to problems, or to fashion unique meanings and connections among concepts in highly original and appreciable or productive ways. Cognitive constructivists are concerned with the question of how creative ideas can be spawned within individual minds. By contrast, social constructionists argue that creativity and innovation depend largely on factors owing to the broader context of socioculturally defined domains of knowledge and practice in which an innovation is conceived, and according to which it is evaluated. Social constructionists look to the institutions and systems of interpersonal relation in which creative ideas can take root, be appreciated by others, and come to achieve prominence.

It seems reasonable to suggest that both individual-cognitive and sociocultural factors enter into creative accomplishment, and that there is merit to be found in both cognitive constructivist and social constructionist perspectives. Human creativity requires an agent. Clearly, creativity involves an individual agent's reflexive ability to conceive of possibilities and constraints. It requires making decisions that lead to contravening or exceeding what has previously been accomplished in an established order, and implementing these decisions through actions. At the same time, however, an agent's creative accomplishment is impeded and abetted by the shared body of sociocultural belief and knowledge that comprises such orders, and in which the agent is enculturated. As we already have discussed, such knowledge and belief enable and constrain one's ability for reflexive consciousness and, in turn, an individual's ability to forge transformations. They provide much of the basis for the generation of new ideas. In addition, creative acts belong to a sphere of public activity, and whether or not something is appreciated as being creative depends on the evaluations expected or given by others knowledgeable of its value.

Despite the seeming importance of both individual-cognitive and sociocultural constituents, little progress has been made in the attempt to situate these considerations in a theoretical framework that elucidates the ways in which individual and sociocultural factors are related, and gives some explanation for how creativity can emerge from them. Some researchers (e.g., Gardner, 1994; Isaksen, Puccio, & Treffinger, 1993; Woodman & Schoenfeldt, 1990) have recognized the need to take into account the multiplicity of individual and sociocultural factors, an insight predated by Rhodes (1961) in his investigative framework of person, product, process, and press. However, a genuine theoretical integration rarely follows this initial recognition. Rather, what one regularly encounters in the literature is the singular, somewhat atheoretical treatment of each of multiple components.

For example, in his biographical study of several well-known major innovators of the modern era, Gardner (1993) identifies a number of contributing factors that he collates and subsumes under three "core elements" or "organizing themes," specifically, the work, the individual, and others. Gardner's approach is for the most part descriptive and taxonomic. His self-proclaimed "anatomy of creativity" does much to delineate the individual and sociocultural ingredients that appear essential to creative accomplishment. However, it does little to elaborate a general theoretical framework that provides an integrative explanation for how such factors may be related and interact, or why this multiplicity of factors is indeed essential.

To his credit, Gardner (1993) does acknowledge the importance of adopting a developmental perspective in comprehending the ways in which innovations are conceived. In what follows, we shall be taking his lead in elaborating the role played by the developmental context in interpreting the conditions of possibility and constraint under which creativity and innovation occur.

Interpreting Creativity and Innovation

We begin with the assertion that creativity is not a vacuous concept. People are able to, and do make judgments about whether or not something or someone is creative. And, often, there is widespread consensus in judgments about the creative merit of certain accomplishments and the individuals responsible for them. Creativity is a significance that is readily recognized despite psychologists' and educators' failing to spell out and agree on a detailed and incontestable formal definition.

We believe that Wittgenstein's (1953) notion of "family resemblance" is relevant here. Wittgenstein argued that a concept does not have an essence or single defining property that ties all the manifestations of it together, and predetermines our interpretations of it. Rather, similar to the way in which members of a human family may resemble one another without being identical or having a singular feature in common, concepts are applied on the basis of our understanding of a network of interconnected similarities and a variety of significant features. A feature or set of features that make a concept applicable in one case may be absent in a subsequent instance. However, another feature belonging to the familial group of features attaching to the concept may now be present and provoke its application. According to Wittgenstein, conceptual understanding is primarily a matter of use—how we actually go about recognizing similarities and relationships—and does not require the specification of exhaustive sets of defining criteria or features. Using the example of games to elaborate his point, Wittgenstein (1953) states:

> Consider for example the proceedings that we call "games." I mean board-games, card-games, ball-games, Olympic games, and so on. What is common to them all?— Don't say: "There *must* be something common or they would not be called 'games'"—but *look and see* whether there is anything common to all.—For if you look at them you will not see something that is common to all, but similarities, relationships, and a whole series of them at that. To repeat: don't think, but look!—Look for example at board-games, with their multifarious relationships. Now pass to card-games; here you find many correspondences with the first group, but many common features drop out, and others appear. When we pass next to ball-games, much that is common is retained, but much is lost.—Are they all 'amusing'? Compare chess with noughts and crosses. Or is there always winning and losing, or competition between players? Think of patience. In ball games there is winning and losing; but when the child throws his ball at the wall and catches it again, this feature has disappeared. ... And we can go through the many, many other groups of games in the same way; can see how similarities crop up and disappear.

And the result is: we see a complicated network of similarities overlapping and criss-crossing: sometimes overall similarities, sometimes similarities of detail. (I, 66)

Wittgenstein's insight into the use of concepts helps to clarify
our understanding of the significance of the term "creativity."
His account illuminates how we recognize instances of creativity without needing a single formal definition, and how the term
is extended in conversational practice to a variety of phenomena
that include both accomplishments and individuals. Further,
Wittgenstein also reveals one basis for the forging of new conceptual connections. An important implication of the notion of
family resemblance is that it is precisely because there is inex-
actitude and a sort of fuzziness in our use of concepts that we
are able to forge new conceptual linkages. As we have mentioned, the notion that creative thought and innovation entail
the forming of new conceptual connections has been acknowledged widely in both traditional and contemporary cognitive
research on creativity.

Beyond the problem of coming to consensus on a formal
definition, which we contend is an issue that largely can be
resolved by taking a Wittgensteinian view toward the nature of
conceptual usage, much of the difficulty psychologists have faced
in comprehending creativity can be traced to a lack of agreement
regarding the location of creativity within individual or sociocultural domains. It is to this issue that we now turn. Our position is that creativity refers to a family of transformations
that, like other emergent psychological phenomena, can only be
comprehended in terms of possibilities and constraints that
emerge from the conditions of psychological underdetermination
and shifting ontology, both of which unfold within the developmental context we have charted in this book.

In focusing on the individual, cognitive constructivists recognize the indissoluble responsibility that an individual agent
bears in the act of creating. Clearly, Rimsky-Korsakov influenced
Stravinsky, and Cézanne's work left a profound mark on Picasso.
As well, public judgments were necessary for these individuals

to receive wide acclaim for their accomplishments. Nonetheless, it was Stravinsky who composed *Le sacre du printemps*, and Picasso who painted *Les demoiselles d'Avignon*. Human creativity requires the actions of individual agents. All creative acts can be seen to involve an agent's transformation of a previously appropriated form of discourse, thought, or action, that has been internalized in his or her memories, personal theories, or embodiment.

Transformations are expressed as creative acts through the agentic decisions made by individuals. Our theories of self are solidified and evolve through the choices we make. At the same time, the decisions we make are largely rooted in the beliefs and understandings that comprise our self-theories. An individual's personal theory of self is an important enablement for the expression of creative acts. Various beliefs that support one's ability to persevere in the face of opposition, take risks, question assumptions, engage ambiguity, be attentive to opportunities, be consumed by one's work, look for unique conceptual connections, and so forth, are ideological features of an individual's self-theory that permit the possibility of creativity. It is on the basis of such personal understandings and beliefs that one is helped to make the kinds of decisions that lead to creative accomplishment. Certain kinds of reflexive decisions are required to bring about creative accomplishment. The personal beliefs and theories one holds about oneself both make possible and constrain those kinds of decisions.

As we already have discussed, our ability to exercise a degree of agency and self-determination, and the possibility of increasingly sophisticated transformations, emerges from the reflexive processes that come of being able consciously to regulate our agency by means of internalized conversations. As well, the spatiotemporal fluidity manifested by memory and imagination contributes to the underdetermination of the private-individual by the public-collective, enabling us to transform our appropriations of ideas, practices, and experiences in ways that transcend current conventions and orders. Serving as vehicles mediating our appropriations of the sociocultural world, our memories and imaginings, and the spatiotemporal fluidity that emerges in them, not only facilitates the ontological transition of the sociocultural to the psychological, but also provides much of the generative substance for creative transformations. The importance of individuals' reflexive conversations and imagined scenarios (e.g., self-questioning and *Gedanken*—thought experiments) and poignant episodic memories of previous experiences in creative thought is well documented in autobiographical accounts and biographical studies (e.g., Gardner, 1993; Ghiselin, 1952/1985). Thus, personal theories, conversations, memory, and imagination provide enablements and constraints for creative transformations.

Cognitive constructivists, among other individualistically oriented psychological researchers, have done much to explicate the role of recurrent personal beliefs, motivations, personality characteristics, conversational tools such as metaphors and analogies, episodic memories, and imagined scenarios, in the genesis of creative ideations and acts. These factors can be seen to map on to what we have delineated as central considerations (i.e., personal theories, conversations, and memory and imagination) in comprehending privately displayed and individually realized transformations. However, while all creative acts are transformations, not all transformations can be construed as creative acts. It is the evaluative demand in the appraisal of something or someone as creative that brings other dimensions of the developmental context to bear on the interpretation of creativity.

In order for an individual transformation to be called creative, it must manifest both significance and value. In attempts to define creativity, much has been made of the novelty found in many creative accomplishments. However, the criterion of novelty has been assailed on the basis that certain activities may in fact be novel, but simply are undeserving of the label "creative." The prototypic example for the case against the criterion of novelty is a schizophrenic's free associations. The associations may be novel, and perhaps even interesting. However, they lack the kind of value and significance required to call them creative. To be creative, a transformation not only must exhibit novelty or originality, but also must evince value and significance.

As we mentioned previously, the creative merit of an original transformation is assessed in relation to the values (manifested in traditions and conventions of critique) appreciated within the field of endeavor with which the transformation is associated. For example, the value of a scientific theory is weighed with respect to its predictive and explanatory utility. A scientific innovation also may be seen as valuable if it has heuristic fertility, that is, it stimulates new hypotheses for subsequent research. As well, the value of a scientific theory may owe to its contribution to a society's industrial progress, or improvement in the health and well-being of its members. In the same light, works of art also must manifest certain kinds of value if they are appropriately to be deemed creative. A work of art may be seen to be of value to the artist if it expresses the feelings the artist wished to convey. Or, on a broader scale, its value may rest on its capacity to inspire others, or capture something of human experience such that others believe the work worthy of inclusion in the cultural heritage. The family of values that contributes to structuring the canons of critique in a domain of endeavor is essential in the designation and authorization of a transformation as creative.

Creativity thus requires recognition of the value of an individual transformation. While the creator may believe that his or her accomplishment has creative significance, it is conceivable that the appraisal may simply be exaggerated or misguided. As well, the creative merit of an accomplishment may not surface until it has been assessed by others in light of considerations not present at the historical point of its conception. Thus, if an individual transformation is to be authorized as creative, it must pass from the domain of the private-individual to the private-collective. It must be published; that is, brought under the light of public scrutiny and subjected to the judgments of others according to the critical canons of the field of endeavor. The expression of the act, and the exposure of others to it, is required if it is to meet the demand of public authorization and to be designated as creative. It is for this reason that the label "creative" has been described as an "honorific" (Young, 1985). Further, if this authorization and designation are attained, the transformation may be conventionalized (cf. Harré, 1984), that is, enshrined amongst the cherished ideas and artifacts of a culture, and maintained in the institutions and collective memory of its members.

Thus, creativity requires evaluation according to sociocultural standards. But, to assert that such evaluations constitute all of which creativity consists is to overemphasize the public-collective at the expense of the private-individual. At the same time, however, to elevate the role of the individual to mythic proportions is to deny the consequence of sociocultural practices and the participation of others in individuals' creative accomplishments. When considered within our own account of psychological development, it becomes clear how creativity resides in both the individual and sociocultural, but how it moves between these domains by virtue of its shifting ontology and underdetermination. The emergence of creative accomplishment may often bring feelings of surprise and strike us with a sense of mystery. However, in light of our theses of shifting ontology and underdetermination, we contend that the emergent and immanent nature of creativity need not lead us to conclude that creativity is as enigmatic and seemingly indescribable as Torrance (1988) and others might contend.

We end this part of our book with a distinction we have taken from Merleau-Ponty (1962) and Charles Taylor (1989a). Intentional consciousness, the ineluctable fact that our experience always is of or about something, is a natural endowment of our embodied agency. Reflexive intentional consciousness is not. For human subjectivity to take its reflexive form, that is for we human agents to conceive of ourselves as subjects or selves, we must be capable of being transformed by our agentic experiences in sociocultural settings. This developmental metamorphosis consists largely in taking up communal conversations and practices as psychological tools with which to think dialogically and responsively. The richer we can make these communal resources, the greater the possibility for productive learning, change, and creative innovation that builds constructively on both the successes and failures of the past.

6

Human Possibility and Constraint

We started this volume by contrasting social constructionist and cognitive constructivist perspectives in psychology, and
holist and atomist positions in contemporary philosophy of social science. The aim of our work has been to present a theory
of psychological development that bridges what we believe are
important insights from these different perspectives. With holists
and social constructionists, we share the view that the psychological emerges from our participation and experience in sociocultural contexts. However, unlike social constructionists, we
consistently have argued that once the psychological unfolds in
the wider context of the pre-existing physical and sociocultural
world, it no longer can be reduced to its largely sociocultural
origins. With atomists and cognitive constructivists, we share an

emphasis on the constructive aspects of human psychology that enable genuine creativity and innovation in human accomplishments and practices. However, unlike cognitive constructivists, we trace the origins of such creative, innovative capabilities to experience in pre-existing sociocultural contexts. Our view is that the psychological is emergent from the sociocultural in interaction with biological and existential givens of individual human life.

At the same time, the sociocultural, in historical terms, is dependent on pre-existing physical and biological domains, and on past contributions of psychological individuals to existing sociocultural forms and practices. In the contexts of collective, historical human experience in the physical world, human societies and cultures gradually have developed and refined unique human capacities for social interaction, including language, as aids to collective and individual survival and development. At any given moment in this history, individual human psychology is simultaneously made possible yet constrained by pre-existing physical, biological, and sociocultural realities. It also is the case that with the emergence of genuine capabilities of reflexivity, individuals go beyond their sociocultural, biological, and physical origins through the exercise of sophisticated, fluid capabilities of imagination and memory, linked to developed theories of self. This underdetermination of more advanced forms of individual human psychology within the developmental context, enables the possibility of further development of the societies and cultures of which such individuals are a part (witness, for example, the far-reaching societal consequences of some creative accomplishments).

In this final part of our book, we want to consider the implications of this general account of psychological and sociocultural ontology and development for modern life. The first part of the chapter is devoted to a further discussion of the relations between the individual and the social that are assumed in our psychology of human possibility and constraint. To illustrate the relevance of our account to contemporary everyday life, we then consider its implications for what Charles Taylor (1991a) has termed the "malaise of modernity." We conclude our book with a summary of our arguments, and what we see as our accomplishments.

THE INDIVIDUAL AND THE SOCIAL

Sociocultural contexts pre-exist us. We are thrown into them at birth and compelled to engage others simply to survive. As embodied agents, the ways in which we learn to think and behave, in the context of development, are largely expressions of our immersion and participation in sociocultural contexts. However, as embodied biological beings, we must deal with existential needs and contexts that are physical and biological as well as sociocultural. The existential basis for subjectivity lies in the fundamental human condition of agency, consisting in a charge to act and in the capacity of embodied agents to execute this charge. While sociocultural contexts shape the expression of human agency, they do not create it. Sociocultural conventions and practices rely on the actions of individuals within them, for their influence on the development of human psychology. This is not just to make the claim that social phenomena would not exist if not for human subjects, but to argue that the reality of the sociocultural depends on the experiences and participations of embodied agents. It is only in the experiences of embodied human agents that sociocultural phenomena can be discerned and made manifest as real. The social exists as a field of possibilities and constraints structured by human agents in their practices and participations. Sociocultural reality consists in human agents acting in terms of their purposes and experiences.

In the course of our development a good deal of what is sociocultural is incorporated into both our prereflective, intentional actions and the more advanced reflexive consciousness that emerges as development unfolds. In the context of development, the social, cultural forms and practices we have internalized become infused with individual intentional agency, eventually giving way to a truly reflexive consciousness capable of transcending these sociocultural legacies, even while constrained by them. When this occurs, we can talk legitimately about a shift in the ontological status of individual psychology, one typified by the transformation from prereflective to reflective forms of human agency and intentionality.

In many ways, our discussions of relations between the sociocultural and the individual follows from Merleau-Ponty's (1962) ontology of human existence, one that eschews sharp contrasts between the individual and the social in favor of existential phenomena such as lived experience and embodied agency. At the same time, we argue that the sociocultural pre-exists the individual, even though the reality of the sociocultural depends on human participation in, and experience of it, both past and present. The historically cumulative sociocultural has a reality that eclipses purely individualized forms of human experience. For example, individual humans participating in a given sociocultural context are constrained in their emergent systems of thought and belief by linguistic, logistic, and related practices in their societies and cultures. Individual human subjects are not free to adopt whatever understandings they wish. It would be dysfunctional for an individual to develop beliefs about things like truth, beauty, honesty, responsibility, and rights, that bore no resemblance to extant forms and practices for such social, cultural, and moral phenomena in her or his society. While it is true that understandings grounded in social, cultural, linguistic, and historical convention may change over time and across societies/cultures, humans are constrained by the norms, understandings, and conventions of their societies. Such understandings and conventions are not especially ephemeral. They have a reality that lies between that of the physical world and more transient aspects of individual thought and belief. It is within these conventions that human psychology emerges and develops. Both sociocultural and psychological phenomena are real in a way that requires each other but is not totally a matter of inescapable, monolithic context.

Psychological ontology changes dynamically in the course of development. Initial forms of individual psychology are manifest as the prereflective embodied agency of human organisms thrown into pre-existing physical and sociocultural contexts. Eventually, many individual humans, through their participation in these contexts, realize psychological possibilities that exceed the constraints of this initial condition. Much of our book has been devoted to the careful charting of this developmental course, especially with respect to the pivotal matters of emergent capacities for forms of memory and imagination that, associated with bona fide theories of self, permit a reflexive intentionality capable of entertaining possibilities not available in the sociocultural features of the developmental context. Such a shift in psychological ontology carries implications for the evolution of sociocultural forms and practices. Through the exercise of human creativity associated with reflexive consciousness and intentionality, possibilities for new sociocultural practices are made available.

The evolution of societies and cultures thus depends on the creative possibilities inherent in the shifting nature of individual psychology, even as individual psychology is enabled and constrained by sociocultural forms and practices. However, unlike the psychological, the sociocultural, even while in dynamic evolution, does not experience a shift in its fundamental nature. For individual humans, the sociocultural always constitutes the sum total of human traditions of accomplishment and practice to this point in history. These traditions are what constrain and mold human psychology, and they are dependent on human sociocultural participation for their own realization, existence, and evolution. At any given moment in human history, sociocultural traditions can act as realistic constraints on the creative innovations issuing from the kind of shifting individual psychological development we have charted. Thus, individual realizations of psychological possibilities always are set against sociocultural traditions and must somehow be seen to advance or significantly modify these traditions if they are to be influential in shaping evolving forms and practices in human societies and cultures.

One way of capturing the foregoing sense of relations between the individual and the social in our theory of psychological development is again to invoke Gadamer's (1960/1975) concept of *Bildung*. Bildung describes the process through which individuals and societies enter an increasingly widely defined community. The cultured individual is one capable of placing individual experience and concerns within a larger perspective or horizon. Similarly, the *Gebildete* culture is one that understands its place within a larger world community.

> To the extent that individuals and cultures integrate this understanding of others and of the differences between them within their own self-understanding, to the extent, in other words, that they learn from others and take a wider, more differentiated view, they can acquire sensitivity, subtlety and a capacity for discrimination. These virtues do not indicate only that a Gebildete culture has appropriated a certain set of beliefs that it finds more defensible than certain others. In becoming cultured we do not simply acquire better norms, values, etc. We also acquire the ability to acquire them. In other words we learn tact, taste and judgment. Perhaps we cannot codify what we have learned as a method for adjudicating between beliefs; nonetheless, through the historical experience in conversation with others that are part of our self-formation or Bildung we can learn to think. And this practical reason thus substitutes for the dogma of the enlightened. (Warnke, 1987, p. 174.)

In the foregoing attempt to clarify Gadamer's philosophical position with respect to the possibilities of individual and social progress, Warnke (1987) maintains that our collective historical and sociocultural situatedness while limiting and constraining what we can know, also teaches us to remember and integrate what we must not forget. This same view, one that we regard as entirely compatible with the kind of theory we have presented, also figures in Charles Taylor's (1991a) consideration of challenges and possibilities inherent in modern life. For Taylor, as for Gadamer and us, sociocultural traditions not only give rise to human psychology, without entirely determining it, but they also can be used to assess new possibilities issuing from human psychological transcendence. The use of traditions as pragmatic, nondogmatic warrants that are not entirely dismissive of innovations and changes, counters the kind of strong relativism and nihlism many associate with the subjectivism of modern life (e.g., Saul, 1995). However, the use of traditions in this way requires a particular kind of ethical attitude and commitment to understanding through dialogical activity and exchange.

GADAMER'S PERSPECTIVISM AND THE ETHICS OF DIALOGICAL UNDERSTANDING

As we already have seen, for Gadamer, all forms of understanding obtain from an inescapable historical and contextual vantage point that assumes a tradition of understanding. Those who would understand never can free themselves from the way of life in which they are embedded. There is no outside vantage point, complete with its own set of ahistorical, universal, and absolute standards, from which to make judgments concerning the relative merits of different interpretations. A single, definitive interpretation is impossible. However, Gadamer's genius has been to recognize that this does not necessarily signal a descent into an epistemic anarchy that abandons any vestige of objectivity.

When interpretations differ, it is because they are drawn from different historical, sociocultural traditions, including the forms of collective and individual psychology emergent within these traditions. Traditions, in Gadamer's sense, are historically effected forms of life that include socioculturally sanctioned conventions, means, and practices. Our psychologies grow out of our participation, given the unique kinds of biological beings we are, in these pre-existing ways of life. We literally embody the traditions in which we are embedded, and extend and alter them by our experiences and actions, initially as prereflective, and eventually as genuinely reflective and reflexive agents.

The nonabsolutist objectivity of interpretations derives from the necessary groundedness of interpreters and interpretations in particular historical modes of existence and practical understanding. All such perspectival objectivity is tied to the horizon of the contemporary sociocultural context within which interpretation occurs. It is a negotiated and negotiable, temporally contingent objectivity that, like the sociocultural horizons invoked, always is subject to ongoing change. Gadamer's metaphor for moving beyond any impasse in interpretative understanding is the "fusion of horizons." He rejects radical incommensurability between competing traditions, and posits the possibility of fusions that result from authentic attempts to understand one's own and others' interpretations and the traditions in which they are embedded. When dialogue across interpretative traditions is honestly and seriously engaged, some degree of fusion is inevitable. The understanding that results will differ, at least somewhat, from that contained in either of the competing traditions, both in its substantive claims and warrants of justification.

In is very important to recognize that Gadamer's depiction of understanding as participating in an occurrence of tradition, or traditions in the case of dialogical fusions, rules out radical subjectivity. As Grondin (1994,) states, "Understanding . . . is less an action of autonomous subjectivity than participating in an event of tradition, a process of transmission in which past and present are constantly mediated" (pp. 116–117). What strikes interpreters as sense or nonsense depends on the traditions in which they are embedded, and these traditions, while always contingent, are accessible in a way that can warrant a kind of perspectival, fallibilist objectivity. Every genuine attempt to understand requires an interpreter to penetrate her or his own preunderstanding and to be open to the understanding of the other. Both of these undertakings are substantive in a way that includes but goes beyond the subjectivity of interpreters. In Gadamer's philosophical hermeneutics, there is no principle higher than dialogue, the dialectic of question and answer. What we draw upon in reflection on our own historically-effected understanding and our efforts to extend it, is the necessarily perspectival, but nonarbitrary, warranted reason that flows from our historical and sociocultural situatedness.

Depending on the sources one consults, Gadamer's philosophical hermeneutics is portrayed variously: sometimes as a

form of Continental, antiphilosophical postmodernism, sometimes as the invitation to dialogue that we have been discussing.
While we believe that most Gadamerian scholars would reject
the first of these views, it is important to note at least two
important criticisms that have been leveled against Gadamer's
ideas. One criticism is that Gadamer's fusion metaphor requires
a form of consensual agreement that reinstates classical ideas of
communicative transparency, or at least fails adequately to
problematize this particular cornerstone of Western, rational bias.
The other is that Gadamer's reliance on tradition is simply another form of foundationalist oppression of marginalized voices.
We want briefly to argue against these criticisms. However, to
do so effectively, we think one must admit that Gadamer does
rely on a kind of ethical stance that cuts across various traditions. In particular, as we soon will argue, the neo-Gadamerian
critical hermeneutics of individuals like Fay (1996) and Kögler
(1996), at least to us, presupposes a strong valuing of understanding as a means of extending the possibilities and boundaries of
human experience.

By seeming to equate successful hermeneutic understanding
with dialogic consensus, Gadamer is not precluding disagreement or the formation of oppositional opinion. He also is not
insisting on agreement with tradition as the ultimate goal of
understanding or the criterion of successful understanding in a
way that renders his perspectivism necessarily conservative. In
equating hermeneutic understanding with dialogical consensus,
Gadamer simply intends to convey the inevitability of the mediation between past and present, alien and familiar, self and
other that is the hallmark of any sincere attempt to understand.
As Warnke (1987) makes clear:

> On this reading, hermeneutic [understanding and encounter]
> can include disagreement: we simply agree to disagree. Al-
> though we cannot break out of the tradition to which we
> belong, we can break with it on any given issue by empha-
> sizing other elements of the tradition, showing the way in
> which the older opinion has to be modified in light of the

way the evidence now looks to us, and so on. In this case our agreement with the tradition consists in the fact that we can justify our new opinion only by coming to terms with its counter-position and understanding in just what way we do disagree with it. (p. 103)

In Charles Taylor's (1991a) terms, Gadamer is emphasizing that:

Things take on importance against a background of intelligibility . . . a horizon. It follows that one of the things we can't do, if we are to define ourselves significantly, is to suppress or deny the horizon against which things take on significance for us. This is the kind of self-defeating move frequently being carried out in our subjectivist civilization. (p. 37)

Thus, in dialogic consensus, the truth that is achieved is necessarily perspectival, but may involve disagreement as much as agreement. The resultant fusion preserves the position of the interpreter and that of the other in a newly emergent stage of the relevant traditions that cancels out previously held positions as adequate on their own. We always agree with tradition in the sense that we are part of it, that is, constituted and oriented by it. However, we inevitably modify tradition in seeking the truth of the matters with which we are concerned, and in assessing truth claims in light of norms and principles inherited from tradition, and fused with those emanating from other perspectives. For Gadamer, hermeneutics is a form of justification that involves the dialogical adjudication of both beliefs and standards of rationality. However, unlike say, Hegel, Gadamer is adamant that any such advances in understanding cannot be foreclosed by anticipating an endpoint of absolute knowledge. For Gadamer, understanding is ever-emergent.

Let us turn now directly to the ethical sense that pervades the Gadamerian dialogue. For Gadamer, successful hermeneutic understanding requires, even demands, the extension of an honest, open, and potentially self-critical "good will" to the other (the text, the conversational partner, the actions or events to be understood). Two very recent attempts to elaborate a neo-Gadamerian, critical hermeneutics explicitly acknowledge the ethical vision required for the kind of critical penetration of one's own preunderstanding and the ongoing, open dialogical encounter that Gadamer promotes.

In his fallibilist account of critical intersubjectivity, Brian Fay (1996) conceives of objectivity as an ongoing dialogue among rival inquirers who attempt to understand each other in a manner genuinely open to the possibility that the other view may have merit, even beyond that of one's own. Such a dialogue requires the systematic examination of rival accounts and methods in a carefully probing, open-minded way. Objectivity thus becomes "a feature of co-operative conversations bent on collectively exploring the worth of various theories and modes of inquiry from a detached (but not necessarily disinterested) perspective" (p. 213). Critical intersubjectivity, as a fallibilist form of objectivity, does not require the abandonment of preconceptions, nor does it imply absolute truth or betoken necessary agreement. It does, however, require the serious attempt to understand through the critical penetration of one's own preunderstanding, and an openness to the understandings of others in dialogical fashion.

Clearly, Fay sees the hermeneutic commitment to understanding in ethical, as well as epistemic terms. When he speaks of the activity of social scientists, including psychologists, he suggests they inevitably work with traditions of discourse that equip them with the conceptual resources needed to do their work. These traditions are not closed, static, or immune to internal and external criticism. If the requisite ethic is in place, social scientists yield to the better argument even when it is counter to their preconceptions and value commitments. They do so by seeking evidence for conclusions, submitting work to outside evaluation, responding honestly to criticism, and in general attempting to be fair in the conduct of their work. In all this, they strive to be self-consciously critical of their conceptions of evidence and standards of significance by taking into account the ways in which their investigations are positioned historically, socially, and politically. They are accountable for the intellectual and evaluative commitments in their work, including responsibility to those who are written for and about. In Fay's own words, "This accountability is satisfied when social analyses acknowledge their positionality vis-à-vis other investigators, their audience, and those under study, and when these other voices are given some active role to play in social analyses themselves" (p. 219).

A similar ethical sense runs through the recent attempt by Hans Herbert Kögler (1996) to fuse important insights from the works of both Gadamer and Michel Foucault. However in Kögler's critical hermeneutics neither truth nor self-reflexive subjectivity is equated with power. Power relations are rather to be seen "as a structured and structuring influence on categorical and theoretical forms of our self-understanding and, consequently on the modes of self-relations that go hand in hand with them, though without reducing these phenomena to power relations per se" (p. 255). Kögler leaves no doubt that ethical principles such as recognition of the "cosubjectivity of the other and the inalienable right to pursue one's self realization" (p. 275) inform his conception of interpretative understanding. Such an ethical vision is indispensable to Kögler's attempt to develop a model of critical interpretative dialogue in which genuine respect for the other, and the possibility of extending one's own understanding and self-realization, are reconciled through a situated, yet not power-blind, form of reflexivity. As we previously have noted (see footnote 19), we agree with Kögler's argument that such values, and the critical practices of self-distanciation that flow from them, are essential to safeguard necessary dialogical openness to other perspectives, and to guard against premature, uncritical assimilation of other traditions to those traditions constitutive of one's own sociocultural, historical preunderstanding.

A PSYCHOLOGY OF POSSIBILITY AND CONSTRAINT IN MODERN TIMES

In his 1991 book, *The Malaise of Modernity*, Charles Taylor examines seemingly intractable conflicts between the demands of modern individuals for authentic self-fulfillment and the requirements of societies for some kind of common good around which to organize sociocultural and political life. Taylor takes as his project the attempt to uncover traditional sources of authenticity, in an attempt to place what he views as more legitimate sources of the ideal of individual authenticity alongside what he considers the less positive sources of this ideal that are widely manifest in contemporary living. Taylor sees contemporary demands for authentic self-fulfillment as springing from the idea that each of us has an original way of being human. Originating in the late eighteenth century, this idea assumes that there is a certain way of being human that is unique to each human individual. Further, it is a moral responsibility for a human individual to discover and live life in this way, and not in imitation of anyone else. Not only is conformity with external demands and standards to be resisted, but the sole legitimate source for authentic self-fulfillment is to be found within an individual's own experiencing and sense-making. Being true to oneself means discovering one's originality, as distinct from anything extant in one's society and culture.

In modern society, many people feel called upon to pursue authentic self-fulfillment, even if this means sacrificing relationships with others and abdicating positions of care (e.g., with respect to children) and responsibility. Enabling of the contemporary move to self-fulfillment, is the adoption of a neutral liberalism, a kind of solipsism, with respect to questions of what constitutes proper conduct and the good life. Essentially, this moral subjectivism in our culture embraces the view that morality cannot be grounded in reason or in the nature of things, but ultimately is an expression of our own self-interest. On this view, reason cannot adjudicate moral disputes or conflicting societal activities conducted in the name of self-interest. Unlike many critics of contemporary culture who have attacked the narcissism and self-serving nature of self-fulfillment and authenticity (e.g., Bloom, 1987), Taylor is not dismissive of the ideal of authenticity, even while disparaging of some of its more or less debased practices. His project is to recover the motivating ideals behind the notion of authenticity, in the hope that these sociocultural traditions can be set against current practices to encourage and persuade moderns to understand and seek authenticity in ways more compatible with shared notions of the common good.

In so doing, Taylor adopts the Gadamerian idea of fused horizons, and provides a case illustration of the kind of sociocultural, individual interaction we envisioned toward the beginning of this final part of our book. Most instructive for our purposes is the following argument of Taylor (1991a).

> The agent seeking significance in life, trying to define his- or herself meaningfully, has to exist in a horizon of important questions. That is what is self-defeating in modes of contemporary culture that concentrate on self-fulfillment *in opposition* to the demands of society, or nature, which shut out history and the bond of solidarity. These self-centered "narcissistic" forms are indeed shallow and trivialized; they are "flattened and narrowed" as Bloom says. But this is not because they belong to the culture of authenticity. Rather it is because they fly in the face of its requirements. To shut out demands emanating beyond the self is precisely to suppress the conditions of significance and hence to court trivialization. To the extent that people are seeking a moral ideal here, this self-immuring is self-stultifying; it destroys the condition in which the ideal can be realized. (p. 40)

Here Taylor is arguing that properly understood, the ideal of authenticity should not be cast as the enemy of all that emanates from beyond the self. Properly understood, authenticity is an ideal that presupposes exactly such demands.

Taylor supports his conclusion by arguing that the uncritical tolerance of all forms of self-expression that abounds in contemporary culture gives undue force to a general subjectivism about value. Things are seen to have significance only when individuals deem them to have such significance, as though individuals exist outside of sociocultural traditions and are capable of granting status to sociocultural entities in a detached, god-like manner. Taylor argues that such a view is "crazy," pointing out that one individual simply does not decide that "the most significant action is wiggling my toes in warm mud," and have the rest of society fall in line with this claim. He goes on to argue that without any explanation for such claims, acceptable to at least some segment of one's society, there can be no basis for distinguishing individual whims and feelings from matters of legitimate social significance. One's feelings never constitute sufficient grounds for respecting one's position because one's feelings cannot determine what is significant.

It is precisely in its failure to differentiate between personal whim and accepted, reasoned social practice (on the assumption of explicit and invoked sociocultural traditions of reason and argument) that the kind of invidious relativism implicit and explicit in the more degenerative social practices of authenticity self-destruct. Like Gadamer (1960/1975), Taylor makes it clear that things take on importance only against a background of intelligibility, a horizon or tradition of sociocultural practice. It follows that if one is to define oneself in a significant way, such definition cannot suppress or deny the horizons or traditions that imbue things with significance. Thus, self-fulfillment cannot be undertaken in isolation from, and ignorance of, the very sociocultural traditions, practices, and forms that it requires.[20]

---

20 This is a point that perhaps deserves special emphasis within that portion of contemporary society overly influenced by certain ideas about self/personal development and psychotherapeutic change that place a strong emphasis on psychological empathy, construed as the idea that significant, authentic forms of self-understanding may be fostered by others' (e.g., psychotherapists, friends, colleagues, coaches, spouses) attempts to adapt the "world views" of individuals as a means of assisting those individuals to better understand themselves. From the perspective advanced herein, any possible value of psychological empathy for fostering genuine self-understanding will not be realized unless such empathy is joined with a kind of supportive, yet also critical, interpretative intersubjectivity that asks individuals to take seriously "other world views," and as a result of such genuine consideration, to elaborate, develop, and better understand their own theories of self and world in a more authentic manner.

Just as we have argued that human psychology cannot be understood outside of the sociocultural practices and forms into which individual humans are thrown at birth and navigate as embodied agents, Taylor argues that psychological development (e.g., self-fulfillment) cannot be understood outside of its proper historical traditions. Both for us and for Taylor, individuals and societies require each other for definition. Psychology is not free to develop in any ways whatsoever. Even in its emergent, reflexive forms, forms replete with possibilities for transcending some of the constraints of human societies and cultures, human psychology still requires a horizon of social and cultural tradition for its functioning and intelligibility. Again, in the words of Jerome Bruner (1996), "to sneer at the power of culture to shape man's mind and to abandon our efforts to bring this power under human control is to commit moral suicide" (pp. 184–185).

Contemporary cultural psychology sometimes has adopted overly strong social constructionist viewpoints, some of which (e.g., Lyotard, 1987) take decidedly postmodern turns by claiming that no form of human practice (e.g., psychology or any other human activity or inquiry) can legitimize itself by attempting to escape from the inevitably situated, contextualized, perspectival nature of all human experience through appeal to anything outside of highly localized sociocultural settings. Such strong relativism holds that we must be content with an epistemic condition characterized by a fundamental incommensurability of many different language games whose differences preclude any possibility of objective knowledge. As we have argued earlier, on this view, there is no common ground for the adoption of more general traditions that might warrant consensus or agreement among different interpretations through the kinds of dialogical encounters championed by Gadamer (1960/75), Kögler (1996), and Taylor (1991b). In contrast, Lyotard's (1987) postmodernism abandons any attempt to arrive at agreement concerning the construction and warranting of understanding and knowledge in a society, because such attempts never can bridge local contexts. They inevitably represent ideologies that reflect only particular sociopolitical and ethnocentric interests.

Postmodernists like Lyotard (1987), in common with sociologists within the strong program of sociology of knowledge
(e.g., Barnes, 1977), thus endorse a kind of epistemological relativism that views any attempt to assess merits of claims outside
of entirely local contexts and conversations as doomed to failure. A major difficulty with such a strong relativism, wedded to
a very narrow and insistent form of social constructionism, arises
in consideration of why anyone should find arguments for it
convincing. After all, does not such a strongly relativistic conclusion itself constitute a kind of totalizing, universal judgment
on any knowledge enterprise or any social practice whatsoever?
Why should one accept this conclusion? What if one or more of
the pluralistic, narrow-gauge, sociocultural language games with
which Lyotard tells us we must live rejects exactly this conclusion? For example, is it really the case that one must accept an
individual's or a social group's views and practices if they are
found to be reprehensible within larger traditions of human
sociocultural practice and accomplishment. Postmodernists like
Lyotard, like modern individuals in pursuit of the more debased
forms of self-fulfillment and authenticity that Taylor decries,
eventually hoist themselves on their own petard of self-reference
and self-interest. They offer little to enrich the broader horizon
of human sociocultural and psychological possibility, because
they insist on being isolated from other sociocultural and psychological traditions. At the same time, they are entirely unrealistic with respect to necessary constraints on local theorizing
and practice.

What we believe is required in face of both challenges of
individual subjectivism and radically postmodern forms of relativism, is a perspective on the individual within society that
acknowledges the kinds of relation between individual psychology and sociocultural sources that we have attempted to detail
in our theory of psychological emergence and development. We
believe that our theory of psychological development is primarily an attempt to explain the way in which the individual
emerges psychologically within the context of social, cultural
practices and forms of historical understanding, and becomes

capable of contributing new possibilities to these sociocultural traditions, even while constrained by them. Biological and existential givens of human existence operate in conjunction with sociocultural traditions in the creation of individual human psychology. Individual human psychology inevitably sows the seeds of new conventions and practices that over time are capable of altering the sociocultural framework itself. However, unlike the more unidirectional ideas of social constructionists or cognitive constructivists in psychology and related disciplines, relationships between the psychological and sociocultural are complex and dynamically interactive, and take place not only contemporaneously but within long-standing and ongoing traditions of human sociocultural and psychological life.

CONCLUDING COMMENT

Our original thesis concerning the shifting ontological status of individual psychology, within the broader developmental and sociocultural contexts we have described, provides a new and dynamic metaphysics. Our theory of psychological development rejects the static, set dualisms of Descartes (1637/1960, 1641/1960) and his followers.[21] In our ontology of human existential givens, we rejected the idea of an initial separation of human

---

21 In this respect, we understand our theory of the individual and society to have much in common with Heidegger's (1949) theory of human Dasein, especially in its authentic mode. Heidegger held that every human is thrown at birth into a pre-existing physical and sociocultural world and is completely shaped by his or her culture. Others who interact with the child create behaviors within the child that eventually form what one would call a person. Only when a newborn has been formed by its environment in this way does it become a Dasein (that entity that each of us is, and which includes inquiring as one of the possibilities of its Being). When a Dasein's inquiry into its Being moves beyond undifferentiated, inauthentic modes of being-in-the-world, and confronts the possibility of nothingness, it becomes a being-toward-death. With this transformation, and the taking of responsibility for one's life that accompanies it, the entire relationship between Dasein and the sociocultural and physical world is transformed. Given that

psychology from its sociocultural context, but subsequently we argued strongly for possibilities of sociocultural innovation and change resident in an emergent, dynamic dualism, one that acknowledges a gradual and graduated separation of individual psychology from its largely sociocultural determinants within the developmental context we painted. Major features of this gradually emergent psychology include the internalization of conversational and relational forms and practices as psychological tools, the acquisition and construction of personal theories (especially theories of self), and the emergence of highly sophisticated reflexive capabilities of memory and imagination. Our joint theses of underdetermination and shifting psychological ontology capture the determined, yet nonreductive nature of these developmentally emergent psychological phenomena. We also have shown how our ontological position concerning the psychological and its development carries significant implications for enhanced understanding of psychotherapy, education, creativity, and psychological inquiry itself. In all these areas, we argued that individual human

---

Dasein, not the sociocultural and physical worlds, is responsible for its own death, it becomes responsible for its own life. Heidegger calls this transformation "care." In caring, Dasein makes the most of its own possibilities, even if these possibilities are originally defined by one's society and culture. Thus, unlike Sartre and other existentialists who championed an autonomous self, defined only by actions and capable of radical freedom (given the meaninglessness of the world), Heidegger was steadfast in defending an emergent, authentic Dasein that required and retained kinships with the sociocultural world for both its existence and development. Our theory does not emphasize classic existential themes in the manner of Heidegger. However, in the relations it assumes between the individual and society, especially with respect to the developmentally emergent possibility for psychological transformation, our theory and Heidegger's have something in common. Both insist on a rejection of Cartesian psychological metaphysics, but in a way that does not preclude the possible realization (emergence) of genuine individual psychology, a psychology determined, but not entirely constrained by sociocultural forms and practices. Of course, unlike Heidegger who held out the promise of such an individual psychology only to those capable of authentic being-toward-death, we maintain that the kind of psychological development we have charted occurs to greater or lesser extents in the lives of most human individuals.

accomplishments need to be understood within the larger framework of historical, sociocultural traditions that affect both collective and individual existence and experience at this point in our history. In this final part of our book, we have attempted to make more explicit the general approach that we have taken in this regard, and attempted to position our account of the development of individual psychology within this broader, necessary framework.

There is a sense in which our work itself illustrates the kind of neo-Gadamerian epistemological fusion we discussed in the third part of our book. Our metaphysical position, dynamic interactionism, adopts important insights of postmodern social constructionism with respect to the etiology of individual psychology. However, out of respect for the phenomenological, epistemic, and possibly causal significance of human psychological experience, it curbs the excesses of postmodern social constructionism's reductive strategy (by which the psychological is reduced to the sociocultural and/or treated only as epiphenomenal). Dynamic interactionism thus fuses postmodern social constructionism with positions that argue for the retention of bona fide psychological phenomena that are not reducible to sociocultural means. The resultant fusion requires an ontological position of emergent, dynamic psychological realism, grounded in an evolving sociocultural realism. Epistemologically, a neo-Gadamerian hermeneutics seems useful in adjudicating fusions of sociocultural traditions, and of sociocultural traditions with the beliefs and actions of psychological individuals.

Dynamic interactionism, with these ontological and epistemological frameworks in place, succeeds in resolving many of the problems that have been attributed to dualism. It does so by reattributing these problems to dualism's assumption of fixed ontologies for the psychological and the sociocultural. It then shows how these ontological assumptions might be challenged and replaced with an ontological position that places the origins of the psychological in the sociocultural, but refuses to reduce the former, once emergent, to the latter. With such an emergent psychological realism in place, there is no need to deny psychology itself in order to avoid metaphysical and epistemological difficulties associated with radically dualistic psychologies.

Postmodern social constructionists are right to be concerned about the difficulties they recognize in radically dualistic psychologies. However, their solution amounts to a denial of the phenomenological, epistemic, and possibly causal significance of psychological phenomena. By placing individual psychology in a unique ontological and epistemological relation to sociocultural traditions, dynamic interactionism avoids conflating psychological experience with its origins, but also insists that it be assessed in relation to the sociocultural traditions from which it springs.

When postmodern social constructionists like Gergen (1994) ask why we are unwilling to explain psychological phenomena, such as individuals' autobiographical accounts of their past experience, in the same social terms that we use to explain manners, dress, or religion, we state emphatically that one's manner, dress, or religion are not the same as one's experiences of, or reasons for choosing or engaging, them. Just because human psychological phenomena are necessarily contingent in their constitution and expression does not mean that their existence necessarily is suspect. Indeed, quite the opposite is the case. Human psychological experience is not to be dismissed, but to be understood and celebrated in full recognition of both its sociocultural origins and the constrained, transcendent possibilities it contains.

In the final analysis, our work in this volume might best be described as an attempt to explain the development of truly psychological phenomena (reflexive intentionality, genuine autobiography, selfhood) in ways that provide them with all the richness of our vast, historical, sociocultural heritage as humans at this point in the evolution of our societies and cultures, yet with the potential to realize heretofore unrecognized and undeveloped possibilities within those developed and developing sociocultural traditions. Our denouement is that the psychology of human possibility and constraint we have described has no Hegelian end in sight, so long as we humans and our societies and cultures continue to unfold.

What man that sees the ever-whirling wheel
Of Change, the which all mortal things doth sway,
But that thereby doth find, and plainly feel,
How Mutability in them doth play

> Edmund Spenser (*The Faerie Queen*, 1596,
> bk. 7 canto 6, st.1)

References

Adler, A. (1963). *The practice and theory of individual psychology*. Paterson, NJ: Littlefield, Adams.

Alpers, S. (1988). *Rembrandt's enterprise: The studio and the market*. Chicago: University of Chicago Press.

Amabile, T. (1983). *The social psychology of creativity*. New York: Springer-Verlag.

Appiah, A. (1989). *Necessary questions: An introduction to philosophy*. Englewood Cliffs: Prentice-Hall.

Bakhtin, M. M. (1986). *Speech genres and other late essays* (V. W. McGee, trans.). Austin: University of Texas Press.

Barnes, B. (1977). *Interests and the growth of knowledge*. London: Routledge & Kegan Paul.

Barone, D. F., Maddux, J. E., & Snyder, C. R. (1997). *Social cognitive psychology: History and current domains*. New York: Plenum.

Barron, F. (1969). *Creative person and creative process*. New York: Holt, Rinehart & Winston.

Barthes, R. (1977). *Roland Barthes* (R. Howard, trans.). New York: Hill & Wang.

Bartlett, F. C. (1932). *Remembering: A study in experimental and social psychology*. Cambridge, MA: University Press.

Basadur, M., & Thompson, R. (1986). "Usefulness of the ideation principle of extended effort in real world professional and managerial creative problem solving." *Journal of Creative Behavior*, 20, 23–34.

Bauersfeld, H. (1988). "Interaction, construction, and knowledge: Alternative perspectives for mathematics education." In T. Cooney & D. Grouws (eds.), *Effective mathematics teaching* (pp. 27–46). Reston, VA: National Council of Teachers of Mathematics & Lawrence Erlbaum.

Beck, A. T. (1967). *Depression: Clinical, experimental and theoretical aspects.* New York: Hoeber.

———. (1976). *Cognitive therapy and the emotional disorders.* New York: International Universities Press.

Berne, E. (1961). *Transactional analysis in psychotherapy.* New York: Grove.

Bevan, W. (1991). "Contemporary psychology: A tour inside the onion." *American Psychologist, 46,* 475–483.

Bloom, A. (1987). *The closing of the American mind.* New York: Simon and Schuster.

Boden, M. A. (1990). *The creative mind.* New York: Basic Books.

———. (1994). "What is creativity?" In M. A. Boden (ed.), *Dimensions of creativity* (pp. 75–117). Cambridge, MA: Bradford/ MIT Press.

Bourdieu, P. (1980/1990). *The logic of practice* (R. Nice, trans.). Stanford CA: Stanford University Press. (Original work published 1980)

Brannigan, A. (1981). *The social basis of scientific discoveries.* Cambridge, England: Cambridge University Press.

Bricker, D., Young, J. E., & Flanagan, C. M. (1993). "Schema-focused cognitive therapy." In K. T. Luehlwein & H. Rosen (eds.), *Cognitive therapies in action* (pp. 88–124). San Francisco: Jossey-Bass.

Brown, J. S., Collins, A., & Duguid, P. (1989). "Situated cognition and the culture of learning." *Educational Research, 18,* 32–42.

Bruner, J. (1986). *Actual minds, possible worlds.* Cambridge, MA: Harvard University Press.

———. (1996). *The culture of education.* Cambridge, MA: Harvard University Press.

Buirs, R., & Martin, J. (1997). "The therapeutic construction of possible selves: Imagination and its constraints." *Journal of Constructivist Psychology, 10,* 153–166.

Burr, V. (1995). *An introduction to social constructionism.* London: Routledge.

Cobb, P. (1994). "Where is mind? Constructivist and sociocultural perspectives on mathematical development." *Educational Researcher,* 23(7), 13–20.

———. (1995). "Continuing the conversation: A response to Smith." *Educational Researcher,* 24(6), 25–27.

Confrey, J. (1990). "A review of the research on student conceptions in mathematics, science, and programming." In C. B. Cazden (ed.), *Review of Research in Education* (Vol. 16, pp. 3–55). Washington, DC: American Educational Research Association.

Csikszentmihalyi, M. (1988). "Society, culture, and person: A systems view of creativity." In R. J. Sternberg (ed.), *The nature of creativity: Contemporary psychological perspectives* (pp. 325–329). New York: Cambridge University Press.

———. (1990). *Flow.* New York: Harper Collins.

Danziger, K. (1990). *Constructing the subject: Historical origins of psychological research.* Cambridge, England: Cambridge University Press.

Derrida, J. (1973). *Speech and phenomena* (D. B. Allison, trans.). Evanston, IL: Northwestern University Press. (Original work published 1967)

———. (1978). *Writing and difference* (A. Bass, trans.). Chicago: University of Chicago Press.

Derry, P. A., & Kuiper, N. A. (1981). "Schematic processing and self-reference in clinical depressives." *Journal of Abnormal Psychology,* 90, 286–297.

Descartes, R. (1960). *Discourse on method and Meditations* (L. J. Lafleur, trans.). New York: The Liberal Arts Press. (Original works published in 1637 and 1641)

Dewey, J. (1929). *Experience and nature* (2nd ed.). Chicago: Open Court.

———. (1964). "The way out of educational confusion." In R. D. Archambault (ed.), *John Dewey on education* (pp. 421–426). Chicago: University of Chicago Press. (Original work published 1931)

Dilthey, W. (1977). *Descriptive psychology and historical under-standing* (R. M. Zaner & K. L. Heiges, trans.). The Hague: Martinus Nijhoff. (Original work published 1894)

Dodds, A. E., Lawrence, J. A., & Valsiner, J. (1997). "The personal and the social: Mead's theory of the 'generalized other.' " *Theory and Psychology, 7,* 483–503.

Dryden, W. (1984). *Rational-emotive therapy: Fundamentals and innovations.* Beckenham, Kent: Croom Helm.

Durkheim, E. (1938). *The rules of sociological method.* New York: Free Press.

Ellis, A. (1962). *Reason and emotion in psychotherapy.* Secaucus, NJ: Lyle Stuart.

Epting, F. R. (1984). *Personal construct counseling and psychotherapy.* New York: Wiley.

Fay, B. (1996). *Contemporary philosophy of social science.* Oxford, England: Blackwell.

Feist, G. J. (1991). "Synthetic and analytic thought: Similarities and differences among art and science students." *Creativity Research Journal, 4,* 145–155.

Feixas, G. (1990). "Personal construct theory and the systemic therapies: Parallel or convergent trends." *Journal of Marital and Family Therapy, 16,* 1–20.

Freeman, A. (1993). "A psychosocial approach for conceptualizing schematic development for cognitive therapy." In K. T. Kuehlwein & H. Rosen (eds.), *Cognitive therapies in action* (pp. 54–87). San Francisco: Jossey-Bass.

Freud, S. (1948). "The relation of the poet to day-dreaming." In *Collected papers* (Vol. 4, pp. 173–183). London: Hogarth. (Original work published 1908)

———. (1966). "Remembering, repeating, and working through." In J. Strachey (ed.), *The standard edition of the complete psychological works of Sigmund Freud* (Vol. 12). London: Hogarth. (Original work published 1914)

Gadamer, H.-G. (1975). *Truth and method* (J. C. B. Mohr, trans.) New York: Seabury Press. (Original work published 1960)

———. (1977). *Philosophical hermeneutics* (D. E. Linge, trans.). Berkeley, CA: University of California Press.

Gardner, H. (1993). *Creating minds.* New York: Basic Books.

———. (1994). "The creator's patterns." In M. A. Boden (ed.), *Dimensions of creativity* (pp. 143–158). London: Bradford/MIT Press.

Gergen, K. J. (1985). "The social constructionist movement in modern psychology." *American Psychologist, 40,* 266–275.

———. (1991). *The saturated self: Dilemmas of identity in contemporary life.* New York: Basic Books.

———. (1994). "Mind, text, and society: Self-memory in social context." In U. Neisser & R. Fivush (eds.), *The remembering self: Construction and accuracy in the self-narrative* (pp. 78–104). New York: Cambridge University Press.

Gergen, K. J., & Gergen, M. M. (1988). "Narrative and the self as relationship." *Advances in Experimental Social Psychology, 21,* 17–56.

———. (1991). "Toward reflexive methodologies." In F. Steier (ed.), *Research and reflexivity* (pp. 76–95). Newbury Park, CA: Sage.

Ghiselin, B. (1985). *The creative process: Reflections on invention in the arts and sciences.* Berkeley: University of California Press. (Original work published 1952)

Giddens, A. (1984). *The constitution of society: Outline of the theory of structuration.* Cambridge, England: Polity.

Gigerenzer, G., (1994). "Where do new ideas come from?" In M. A. Boden (ed.), *Dimensions of creativity* (pp. 53–54). Cambridge, MA: Bradford/MIT Press.

Greeno, J. G. (1991). "Number sense as situated knowledge in a conceptual domain." *Journal for Research in Mathematics Education, 22,* 170–218.

Greenwood, J. D. (1989). *Explanation and experiment in social psychological science: Realism and the social constitution of action.* New York: Springer-Verlag.

———. (1991). *Relations and representations: An introduction to the philosophy of social psychological science.* London: Routledge.

Grondin, J. (1994). *Introduction to philosophical hermeneutics* (J. Weinsheimer & D. G. Marshall, trans.) (2nd ed.). New York: Continuum. (Original work published 1960)

Gruber, H. E., & Davis, S. N. (1988). "Inching our way up Mount Olympus: The evolving-systems approach to creative thinking." In R. J. Sternberg (ed.), *The nature of creativity: Contemporary psychological perspectives* (pp. 243–270). New York: Cambridge University Press.

Guidano, V. F. (1987). *Complexity of the self.* New York: Guilford.

———. (1991). *The self in process.* New York: Guilford.

Guilford, J. P. (1950). Creativity. *American Psychologist,* 14, 469–479.

———. (1967). *The nature of human intelligence.* New York: McGraw-Hill.

Guilford, J. P., Wilson, R. C., & Christensen, P. R. (1952). *A factoranalytic study of creative thinking. I. Administration of tests and analysis of results.* Los Angeles: University of Southern California Press.

Habermas, J. (1971). *Knowledge and human interests.* Boston: Beacon Press.

———. (1984). *The theory of communicative action* (T. McCarthy, trans.). London: Heinemann. (Original work published 1981)

Harré, R. (1984). *Personal being: A theory for individual psychology.* Cambridge, MA: Harvard University Press.

Harré, R., & Krausz, M. (1996). *Varieties of relativism.* Oxford, England: Blackwell.

Hartmann, H. (1939). *Ego psychology and the problem of adaptation* (D. Rapaport, trans.). New York: International Universities Press.

Heidegger, M. (1949). *Existence and being* (W. Brock, ed. and trans.). Chicago: Henry Regnery.

———. (1962). *Being and time* (J. Macquarrie & E. Robinson, trans.). New York: Harper & Row. (Original work published in 1927)

Hiebert, J., & Carpenter, J. P. (1992). "Learning and teaching with understanding." In D. A. Grouws (ed.), *Handbook of research on mathematics teaching and learning* (pp. 65–98). New York: Macmillan.

Hoshmand, L. T., & Martin, J. (1995). *Research as praxis: Lessons from programmatic research in therapeutic psychology.* New York: Teachers College Press.

Howard, G. S. (1989). *A tale of two stories: Excursions into a narrative approach to psychology.* Notre Dame, IN: Academic Publications.

———. (1991). "Culture tales: A narrative approach to thinking, cross-cultural psychology, and psychotherapy." *American Psychologist, 46,* 187–197.

———. (1993). "Steps toward a science of free will." *Counseling and Values, 37,* 116–128.

Isaksen, S. G., Puccio, G. J., & Treffinger, D. J. (1993). "An ecological approach to creativity research: Profiling for creative problem solving." *Journal of Creative Behavior, 27,* 149–170.

Johnson-Laird, P. N. (1983) *Mental models: Towards a cognitive science of language, inference, and consciousness.* Cambridge, MA: Harvard University Press.

———. (1988) *The computer and the mind.* Cambridge, MA: Harvard University Press.

Kant, I. (1965). *Critique of pure reason* (N. K. Smith, trans.). New York: St. Martin's. (Original work published in 1787)

Kelly, G. (1955). *A theory of personality: The psychology of personal constructs.* New York: Norton.

Kempen, H. J. G. (1996). "Mind as body moving in space: Bringing the body back into self-psychology." *Theory and Psychology, 64,* 715–731.

Koch, S. (1981). "The nature and limits of psychological knowledge: Lessons of a century qua 'science.'" *American Psychologist, 36,* 257–269.

———. (1993). " 'Psychology' or the 'psychological studies'?" *American Psychologist, 48,* 902–904.

Kögler, H. H. (1996). *The power of dialogue: Critical hermeneutics after Gadamer and Foucault.* (P. Hendrickson, trans.). Cambridge, MA: The MIT Press.

Kris, E. (1952). *Psychoanalytic explorations in art.* New York: International Universities Press.

Kubie, L. (1958). *The neurotic distortion of the creative process.* Lawrence, KA: University of Kansas Press.

Kuhn, T. (1970). *The structure of scientific revolutions* (2nd ed.). Chicago: University of Chicago Press.

Kuiper, N. A., & Higgins, E. T. (1985). "Social cognition and depression: A general integrative perspective." *Social Cognition, 3,* 1–15.

Lagache, E. (1997). "Of ships passing in the night? Social constructionism as a local construction." *Theory and Psychology, 7,* 284–285.

Lakatos, I. (1970). "Falsification and the methodology of scientific research programs." In I. Lakatos & A. Musgrave (eds.), *Criticism and the growth of knowledge* (pp. 91–196). Cambridge, England: Cambridge University Press.

Langley, P., Simon, H., Bradshaw, G. L., & Zytkow, J. M. (1987). *Scientific discovery.* Cambridge, MA: The MIT Press.

Lather, P. (1992). "Postmodernism and the human sciences." In S. Kvale (ed.), *Psychology and postmodernism* (pp. 88–109). Newbury Park, CA: Sage.

Lave, J., & Wenger, E. (1991). *Situated learning: Legitimate peripheral participation.* Cambridge, England: Cambridge University Press.

Liotti, G. (1986). "Structural cognitive therapy." In W. Dryden & W. Golden (eds.), *Cognitive-behavioral approaches to psychotherapy* (pp. 91–128). London: Harper & Row.

Lubeck, S., & Bidell, T. (1988). "Creativity and cognition: A Piagetian framework." *Journal of Creative Behavior, 22,* 31–41.

Lyddon, W. J. (1995). "Forms and facets of constructivist psychology." In R. A. Neimeyer & M. J. Mahoney (eds.), *Constructivism in psychotherapy* (pp. 69–92). Washington, DC: American Psychological Association.

Lyotard, J. F. (1987). "The postmodern condition." In K. Baynes, J. Bohman, & T. McCarthy (eds.), *After philosophy: End or transformation* (pp. 68–93). Cambridge, MA: The MIT Press.

MacKinnon, D. (1962). "The nature and nurture of creative talent." *American Psychologist, 17,* 484–495.

Mahoney, M. J. (1980). "Psychotherapy and the structure of personal revolutions." In M. J. Mahoney (ed.), *Psychotherapy process* (pp. 157–180). New York: Plenum.

———. (1990). *Human change processes.* New York: Basic Books.

———. (1995). "Continuing evolution of the cognitive sciences and psychotherapies." In R. A. Neimeyer & M. J. Mahoney (eds.), *Constructivism in psychotherapy* (pp. 39–68). Washington, DC: American Psychological Association.

Mair, M. (1988). "Psychology as storytelling." *International Journal of Personal Construct Psychology*, 1, 125–138.

Margolis, J. (1991). *The truth about relativism*. Cambridge, MA: Basil Blackwell, Inc.

Markus, H. (1977). "Self-schemata and processing information about the self." *Journal of Personality and Social Psychology*, 35, 63–78.

———. (1983). "Self-knowledge: An expanded view." *Journal of Personality*, 51, 543–565.

Markus, H., & Nurius, P. (1986). "Possible selves." *American Psychologist*, 41, 954–969.

Markus, H., & Wurf, E. (1987). "The dynamics of self-concept: A social psychological perspective." *Annual Review of Psychology*, 38, 296–337.

Martin, J. (1987). *Cognitive-instructional counseling*. London, ON, Canada: Althouse Press.

———. (1993a). "Episodic memory: A neglected phenomenon in the psychology of education." *Educational Psychologist*, 28, 169–183.

———. (1993b). "The problem with therapeutic science." *Journal of Psychology*, 127, 365–374.

———. (1994). *The construction and understanding of psychotherapeutic change: Conversations, memories, and theories*. New York: Teachers College Press.

———. (1996). "Psychological research as the formulation, demonstration, and critique of psychological theories." *Journal of Theoretical and Philosophical Psychology*, 16, 1–18.

Martin, J., & Sugarman, J. H. (1996). "Bridging social constructionism and cognitive constructivism." *Journal of Mind and Behavior*, 17, 291–320.

———. (1997). "Societal-psychological constructionism: Societies, selves, traditions, and fusions." *Journal of Theoretical and Philosophical Psychology*, 17, 120–136.

————. (1998). "Dynamic interactionism: Elaborating a psychology of human possibility and constraint." *Journal of Mind and Behavior*, 19, 195–214.

Martin, J., & Thompson, J. (1997). "Between scientism and relativism: Phenomenology, hermeneutics, and the new realism in psychology." *Theory and Psychology*, 7, 629–652.

McAdams, D. P. (1988). *Power, intimacy, and the life story: Personological inquiries into identity*. New York: Guilford Press.

McNamee, S., & Gergen, K. J. (1992). *Therapy as social construction*. Newbury Park, CA: Sage.

Mead, G. H. (1934). *Mind, self and society*. Chicago: University of Chicago Press.

Meichenbaum, D. (1977). *Cognitive-behavior modification: An integrative approach*. New York: Plenum.

Merleau-Ponty, M. (1962). *Phenomenology of perception* (C. Smith, trans.). London: Routledge & Kegan Paul.

Mobley, M. I., Doares, L. M., & Mumford, M. D. (1992). "Process analytic models of creative capacities: Evidence for the combination and reorganization process." *Creativity Research Journal*, 5(2), 125–155.

Mounce, H. O. (1997). *The two pragmatisms: From Peirce to Rorty*. New York: Routledge.

Much, N. C. (1992). "The analysis of discourse as methodology for a semiotic psychology." *American Behavioral Scientist*, 36, 52–72.

Mumford, M. D., Mobley, M. I., Uhlman, C. E., Reiter-Palmon, R., & Doares, L. M. (1991). "Process analytic models of creative capacities." *Creativity Research Journal*, 4(2), 91–122.

Neimeyer, R. A. (1995). "Constructivist psychotherapies: Features, foundations, and future directions." In R. A. Neimeyer & M. J. Mahoney (eds.), *Constructivism in psychotherapy* (pp. 11–38). Washington, DC: American Psychological Association.

Neimeyer, R. A., & Neimeyer, G. J. (eds.) (1987). *Personal construct therapy casebook*. New York: Springer.

Newman, D., Griffin, P., & Cole, M. (1989). *The construction zone: Working for cognitive change in school.* Cambridge, England: Cambridge University Press.

Newton-Smith, W. H. (1981). *The rationality of science.* London: Routledge & Kegan Paul.

Noppe, L. D. (1985). "The relationship of formal thought and cognitive styles to creativity." *Journal of Creative Behavior,* 19, 88–96.

Noppe, L. D., & Gallagher, J. M. (1977). "A cognitive style approach to creative thought." *Journal of Personality Assessment,* 41, 85–90.

Nozick, R. (1981). *Philosophical explanations.* Cambridge, MA: The Belknap Press of Harvard University.

Nunes, T. (1992). "Ethnomathematics and everyday cognition." In D. A. Grouws (ed.), *Handbook of research on mathematics teaching and learning* (pp. 557–574). New York: Macmillan.

Nuthall, G., & Alton-Lee, A. (1993). "Predicting learning from student experience of teaching: A theory of student knowledge construction in classrooms." *American Educational Research Journal,* 30, 799–840.

———. (1995). "Assessing classroom learning: How students use their knowledge and experience to answer classroom achievement test questions in science and social studies." *American Educational Research Journal,* 32, 185–223.

Oyserman, D., & Markus, H. R. (1990). "Possible selves and delinquency." *Journal of Personality and Social Psychology,* 59, 112–125.

Penn, D. (1985). "Feed-forward: Future questions, future maps." *Family Process,* 24, 299–310.

Pepper, S. C. (1942). *World hypotheses.* Berkeley, CA: University of California Press.

Perkins, D. N. (1981). *The mind's best work.* Cambridge, MA: Harvard University Press.

———. (1988). "The possibility of invention." In R. J. Sternberg (ed.), *The nature of creativity: Contemporary psychological perspectives* (pp. 362–385). New York: Cambridge University Press.

Peters, R. S. (1966). *Ethics and education*. London: Allen & Unwin.

Phillips, D. C. (1995). "The good, the bad, and the ugly: The many faces of constructivism." *Educational Researcher*, 24(7), 5–12.

Piaget, J. (1954). *The construction of reality in the child* (M. Cook, trans.). New York: Basic.

———. (1970). *Genetic epistemology*. New York: Columbia University Press.

Polkinghorne, D. E. (1988). *Narrative psychology*. Albany: State University of New York Press.

———. (1994). "A path for understanding psychology." *Journal of Theoretical and Philosophical Psychology*, 14, 128–145.

Popper, K. (1948). *The open society and its enemies* (4th ed.). London: Routledge & Kegan Paul.

Prawat, R. S. (1993). "The value of ideas: Problems versus possibilities in learning." *Educational Researcher*, 22(2), 5–16.

———. (1995). "Misreading Dewey: Reform, projects, and the language game." *Educational Researcher*, 24, 13–22.

Prawat, R. S., & Floeden, R. E. (1994). "Philosophical perspectives on constructivist views of learning." *Educational Psychologist*, 29, 37–48.

Procter, H. G. (1987). "Change in the family construct system." In R. A. Neimeyer & G. J. Neimeyer (eds.), *Personal construct therapy casebook* (pp. 153–171). New York: Springer.

Pylyshyn, Z. W. (1984). *Computation and cognition*. Cambridge, MA: The MIT Press.

Quinn, E. (1980). "Creativity and cognitive complexity." *Social Behavior and Personality*, 8, 213–215.

Rhodes, M. (1961). "An analysis of creativity." *Phi Delta Kappan*, 42, 305–310.

Robinson, D. N. (1991). "Text, context and agency." *Journal of Theoretical and Philosophical Psychology*, 11, 1–10.

Rosen, S. (1982). *My voice will go with you: The teaching tales of Milton H. Erickson*. New York: Norton.

Rostan, S. M. (1994). "Problem finding, problem solving, and cognitive controls: An empirical investigation of critically acclaimed productivity." *Creativity Research Journal,* 7(2), 97–110.

Sampson, E. E. (1983). *Justice and the critique of pure psychology.* New York: Plenum.

———. (1989). "The deconstruction of self." In J. Shotter and K. J. Gergen (eds.), *Texts of identity* (pp. 1–19). Newbury Park, CA: Sage.

Sarbin, T. R. (1986). *Narrative psychology: The storied nature of human conduct* New York: Praeger.

Sass, L. A. (1992). "The epic of disbelief: The postmodern turn in contemporary psychoanalysis." In S. Kvale (ed.), *Psychology and postmodernism* (pp. 166–182). Newbury Park, CA: Sage.

Saul, J. R. (1995). *The unconscious civilization.* Concord, ON, Canada: Anansi.

Schaffer, S. (1994). "Making up discovery." In M. A. Boden (ed.), *Dimensions of creativity* (pp. 13–51). Cambridge, MA: Bradford/MIT Press.

Shotter, J. (1993). *Conversational realities: Constructing life through language.* London: Sage.

Shotter, J. & Gergen, K. J. (eds.). (1989). *Texts of identity.* Newbury Park, CA: Sage.

Simon, H. (1988). "Creativity and motivation: A response to Csikszentmihalyi." *New Ideas in Psychology,* 6(2), 177–182.

Simonton, D. K. (1988). "Creativity, leadership, and chance." In R. J. Sternberg (ed.), *The nature of creativity: Contemporary psychological perspectives* (pp. 386–426). New York: Cambridge University Press.

Singer, J. A. & Salovey, P. (1993). *The remembered self: Emotion and memory in personality.* New York: The Free Press/Macmillan.

Smith, E. (1995). "Where is the mind? Knowing and knowledge in Cobb's constructivist and sociocultural perspectives." *Educational Researcher,* 24(6), 23–25.

Smith, M. B. (1994). "Selfhood at risk: Postmodern perils and the perils of postmodernism." *American Psychologist,* 49, 405–411.

Smolucha, L., & Smolucha, F. (1992). "Vygotskian theory: An emerging paradigm with implications for a synergistic psychology." *Creativity Research Journal*, 5, 87–97.

Sorell, T. (1991). *Scientism: Philosophy and the infatuation with science*. New York: Routledge.

Sternberg, R. J. (1988). "A three-facet model of creativity." In R. J. Sternberg (ed.), *The nature of creativity: Contemporary psychological perspectives* (pp. 125–147). New York: Cambridge University Press.

Sugarman, J. H. (1995). "Transcendental interpretation: An alternative approach to psychological inquiry." *Journal of Theoretical and Philosophical Psychology*, 15(1), 16–40.

Szasz, T. (1961). *The myth of mental illness*. New York: Harper and Row.

Taylor, C. (1989a). "Embodied agency." In H. Pietersma (ed.), *Merleau-Ponty: Critical essays* (pp. 1–21). Lanham, MD: University Press of America.

———. (1989b). *Sources of the self*. Cambridge, MA: Harvard University Press.

———. (1991a). *The malaise of modernity*. Concord, ON, Canada: Anansi.

———. (1991b). "The dialogical self." In D. R. Hiley, J. F. Bohman, & R. Shusterman (eds.), *The interpretive turn: Philosophy, science, culture* (pp. 304–314). Ithaca, NY: Cornell University Press.

———. (1995). *Philosophical arguments*. Cambridge, MA: Harvard University Press.

Torrance, E. (1962). *Guiding creative talent*. Englewood Cliffs, NJ: Prentice-Hall.

———. (1966). *Torrance tests of creative thinking: Norms-technical manual*. Princeton, NJ: Personnel Press.

———. (1972). "Predictive validity of the Torrance tests of creative thinking." *Journal of Creative Behavior*, 6, 236–252.

———. (1988). "The nature of creativity as manifest in its testing." In R. J. Sternberg (ed.), *The nature of creativity* (pp. 43–75). New York: Cambridge University Press.

Toulmin, S., & Leary, D. E. (1994). "The cult of empiricism in psychology and beyond." In S. Koch & D. E. Leary (eds.), *A century of psychology as a science* (pp. 594–617). Washington, DC: American Psychological Association.

Tulving, E. (1983). *Elements of episodic memory.* New York: Oxford University Press.

Vogel, D. (1994). "Narrative perspectives in theory and therapy." *Journal of Constructivist Psychology, 7,* 243–261.

von Glasersfeld, E. (1987). *The construction of knowledge: Contributions to conceptual semantics.* Seaside, CA: Intersystems Publications.

———. (1989). "Cognition, construction of knowledge, and teaching." *Synthese, 80,* 121–140.

———. (1992). "Constructivism reconstructed: A reply to Suchting." *Science and Education, 1,* 379–384.

———. (1996). "Footnotes to 'the many faces of constructivism.' " *Educational Researcher, 25*(6), 19.

Vygotsky, L. S. (1978). *Mind in society: The development of higher psychological processes.* Cambridge, MA: Harvard University Press.

———. (1986). *Thought and language* (A. Kozulin, trans.). Cambridge, MA: The MIT Press. (Original work published 1934)

Warnke, G. (1987). *Gadamer: Hermeneutics, tradition and reason.* Stanford, CA: Stanford University Press.

Warnock, M. (1994). *Imagination and time.* Oxford: Blackwell.

Weisberg, R. W. (1993). *Creativity: Beyond the myth of genius.* New York: W. H. Freeman & Company.

Wertz, F. J. (1995, August). *The scientific status of psychology.* Paper presented at the meeting of the American Psychology Association, New York.

White, M., & Epston, D. (1990). *Narrative means to therapeutic ends.* New York: Norton.

Williams, R. N. (1992). "The human context of agency." *American Psychologist, 47,* 752–760.

Wittgenstein, L. (1953). *Philosophical investigations.* (G. E. M. Anscombe, trans.). Oxford: Basil Blackwell.

Woodman, R. W., & Schoenfeldt, L. G. (1990). "An interactionist model of creative behavior." *Journal of Creative Behavior*, 24, 10–20.

Young, J. G. (1985). "What is creativity?" *Journal of Creative Behavior*, 19, 77–87.

Zuckerman, H. (1977). *Scientific elite: Nobel laureates in the United States.* New York: Free Press.

Subject Index

Name Index

Adler, A., 75
Alpers, S., 104
Alton-Lee, A., 93–95
Amabile, T., 101
Appiah, A., 48

Bakhtin, M.M., 20–21n. 5
Barnes, B., 129
Barone, D.F., 39n
Barron, F., 100
Barthes, R., 2
Bartlett, F.C., 5, 8, 24n. 8
Basadur, M., 101
Bauersfeld, H., 88
Beck, A.T., 74
Berne, E., 75
Bevan, W., 42
Bidell, T., 102
Bloom, A., 126
Boden, M.A., 100, 101
Bourdieu, P., 32n. 12
Bradshaw, G.L., 101
Brannigan, A., 104
Bricker, D., 72
Brown, J.S., 87
Bruner, J., 37, 75, 91, 128
Buirs, R., 73, 81–82
Burr, V., 12n

Carpenter, J.P., 87
Christensen, P.R., 100
Cobb, P., 90–92
Cole, M., 88
Collins, A., 87
Confrey, J., 87
Csikszentmihalyi, M., 101, 102

Danziger, K., 43
Davis, S.N., 102
Derrida, J., xi, 2, 10, 56
Derry, P.A, 74
Descartes, R., viii, 1–2, 68, 130
Dewey, J., xiv, 39n, 92
Dilthey, W., 43
Doares, L.M., 101
Dodds, A.E., 39n
Dryden, W., 74
Duguid, P., 87
Durkheim, E., 12

Ellis, A., 74
Epston, D., 75
Epting, F.R., 72

Fay, B., 13–14, 30, 34, 62, 121,
    123–124
Feist, G.J., 101

157